3383 8508

W9-BFY-276

FAT QUARTER
QUILTING

WITHDRAWN
BEAVERTON CITY LIBRARY
Beaverton, OR 97005
Member of Washington County
COOPERATIVE LIBRARY SERVICES

Sue Penn

©2006 Sue Penn
Published by

kp books
An Imprint of F+W Publications

700 East State Street • Iola, WI 54990-0001
715-445-2214 • 888-457-2873

Our toll-free number to place an order or obtain a free catalog is (800) 258-0929.

All rights reserved. No portion of this publication may be reproduced or transmitted in any form or by any means, electronic or mechanical, including photocopy, recording, or any information storage and retrieval system, without permission in writing from the publisher, except by a reviewer who may quote brief passages in a critical article or review to be printed in a magazine or newspaper, or electronically transmitted on radio or television.

The following registered trademark terms, companies and products appear in this publication: Olfa®, Omnigrid®, Schmetz™, Sulky®, Lite Steam-A-Seam 2®, Slimline Storage Box™, The Warm™ Company, Steam-A-Seam®, Warm & Natural®.

Library of Congress Catalog Number: 2005922943

ISBN: 0-89689-171-2

Edited by Susan Sliwicki
Designed by Emily Adler

Printed in China

Dedication

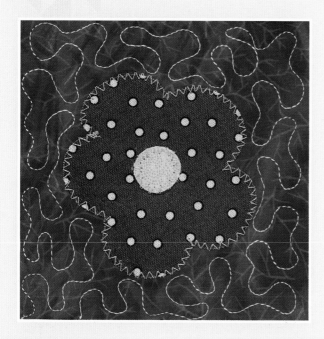

This book is dedicated to my husband, my children and my Heavenly Father. Everything else I do comes second to them. Between stitching projects and writing instructions, I spend my time going to baseball and softball games, cross country and track meets, football and soccer games, wrestling meets, volleyball matches and basketball games. Then there are lessons and concerts for violin, trumpet, flute, drums, piano and voice. I've always said that we wouldn't have a social life without our kids! Thank you, Bob, Lauren, Rob, Jonathan and Nikki for loving me through this book. I love you more than you will ever know!

Acknowledgments

Special thanks to:

• My husband, Bob, for taking over in the last few days as I finished this book and for being an inspiration;

• Roxane Wright, who did all of the beautiful quilting and was ready at the drop of a pin to quilt and bind my projects;

• Debby Sissman of Henry Glass Fabric Co., for supplying much of the wonderful fabric for the projects; and

• Susan Sliwicki, my helpful editor from KP Books.

Without all of you this book wouldn't have been possible. Thank you from the bottom of my heart.

Table of Contents

CHAPTER 1

Learn Terms, Tools and Techniques

I love fat quarters.

I love buying them in bundles, in pairs, all by themselves. I love buying more and more fat quarters. I love stacking and re-stacking, mixing and matching to find if this goes with that. And then, I love starting all over again.

Fat quarters are my inspiration for that next project, and they are better than sliced bread. What would we do without fat quarters?

FAT QUARTERS

What Are Fat Quarters?

Webster's Dictionary does not have a definition for fat quarter. It probably should. There are many more obscure words contained between its covers, and fat quarter is actually a simple term.

A fat quarter is a piece of quilting fabric that is approximately 18" x 22". It is a half yard of fabric cut in half again along the fold. You still have a quarter yard of fabric, but it is "fatter" than the traditional quarter yard cut 9" wide from selvage to selvage. A fat quarter is a much more usable and appealing piece of fabric.

How Many Squares Will a Fat Quarter Yield?

Not all fat quarters are created equal.

I figure that the width is usually at least 18", but the length is sometimes only 20". Have you noticed that our bolts of fabric aren't 44" wide any more? Most are only 42" or 40". So, let's figure that the usable yardage is about 18" x 20". Here's a chart to help you plan for your next fat quarter quilting project.

FAT QUARTER EQUIVALENTS

SIZE OF SQUARE	YIELD
2"	90
2½"	56
3"	36
3½"	25
4"	20
4½"	16
5"	12
5½" or 6"	9
6½"	6
7", 7½", 8" or 9"	4

Where Can Fat Quarters be Found?

Fat quarters can be found in just about every quilt shop in the country. They are the tempting little cuts of fabric often found right by the checkout. They are the rows and rows of folded squares in boxes next to the bolts. They are the beautiful bundles of coordinated collections stacked on the shelves.

If your shop doesn't carry them, the good news is that you can make your own. Just cut a half yard of fabric in half again on the fold. A friend and I sometimes buy a half yard on purpose and split it. It seems like you get twice as much fabric that way.

How Should I Prepare My Fat Quarters?

I have a confession: I usually don't prewash my fabric. I know; the purists are rolling over in their graves. I like the stabilizer in the unwashed fabric, because it makes for easier cutting through the crisp fabric. Rarely have I had to wash a quilt, so I'm not concerned about bleeding and shrinkage, either. All I usually do to get my fat quarters ready for sewing is to press the wrinkles out.

I find that most of the dyes used today are very stable. If I am concerned about a particular fabric, I run the corner of it under warm water to see if it bleeds. If it does, then — and only then — I prewash my fat quarters and other fabric. If you want to wash and dry your fat quarters, go ahead. It really is a personal preference.

BASIC TOOLS AND NOTIONS

Companies constantly are coming up with new tools, notions and supplies to make your sewing and quilting easier and more enjoyable. From sprays to special pins, there are plenty of choices available to make basting easier and more efficient. When it comes to marking, there's everything from pencils and chalks to pens whose inks wash out. Other tools, such as quilter's gloves, mini irons or magnetic pincushions and needle holders, aren't necessities, but you may find that they come in handy. Explore the notions and tools in your favorite shop to discover what you like to use.

Here is a list of basic quilting tools and notions you will use for projects in this book.

• Rotary Cutting Mat: This is a ruled mat designed specifically for use with a rotary cutter. The mat is self-healing, and it doesn't dull the blade. My favorite brand is Omnigrid cutting mats.

• Rotary Cutter: This tool looks like a pizza cutter, but it is really a round razor blade attached to a handle. The most common sizes are 28 mm, 45 mm and 60 mm. The blades are extremely sharp, so be careful! I have heard it said that with the small blade, you can take off a fingernail, with the medium blade, the tip of your finger, and with the large blade, your whole finger.

• Acrylic Rulers: I love my quilting rulers. My favorite is the 6" x 24". If you are only going to purchase one ruler, this is the one to get. It is long enough to cut the whole length of the fat quarter, and narrow enough to cut small squares. I have the whole set of Omnigrid rulers, and they are my favorite.

• Sewing Machine: Your sewing machine is your most important tool. A good, basic machine that runs well is a must. If you have to fight with your machine to get a project done, you won't enjoy it, and you won't be a quilter for long. Can you imagine your husband putting up with a saw or a drill that does a poor job? If you spend the money on a good machine, you never will regret it.

• ¼" Foot: A ¼" foot is a great way to make sure that you get an accurate seam allowance. This foot measures ¼" from the needle to the edge of the foot. See your local sewing machine dealer to pick one up.

• Needles: You will need both hand sewing and machine needles. For hand sewing, use the right needle for the job. For machine sewing, I use Schmetz Universal 80/12 needles. Don't wait for your machine's needle to break before you replace it. Change your sewing machine needle every two or three projects.

• Scissors: Good, sharp sewing scissors are a must. Using your child's school scissors just won't cut it. You need a sharp cutting edge that is free of nicks.

• Iron and Ironing Board: A nice, basic iron and an adjustable ironing board are great. I've used irons with nonstick soleplates and irons without them. I really don't have a preference.

• Seam Ripper: While you do need this tool, you can control how much you need to use it. Remember what they say: "As you shall sew, sew shall you rip!"

• Fusible Web: Lite Steam-A-Seam 2 is an ideal fusible web for most appliqué projects. It is light, it doesn't gum up your needle, and it can't be over-ironed like some fusible webs.

• Thread: I use both 100 percent cotton and cotton-polyester blend thread without any problems. My personal choice for a brand is Metler Metrosene. Medium tan or gray are great neutrals that can be used on almost any project.

• Embroidery Thread: I almost always use Sulky 40-weight rayon. Sulky has an Embroiderer's Dream Package that has a great selection of 104 colors in a Slimline Storage Box. You also can buy the thread by the individual spool.

• Buttons: Three projects in this book use buttons. Covered buttons are metal forms that often are used to create customized fabric-covered buttons for upholstery work, such as those used in the Super Simple Fat Quarter Pillows project. Collections of traditional buttons are used for two other projects in this book: the Button Picture and the Jamming Pajama Tote.

ROTARY CUTTING BASICS

1. Square up the edges to the mat.

2. Place the fat quarter on a large cutting mat with the selvage lined up along a horizontal line.

3. Lay a ruler along the right side. Cut the raw edge perpendicular to the selvage.

4. Flip the fat quarter around and begin cutting your squares and strips from this straightened edge. If you are left handed, reverse these directions.

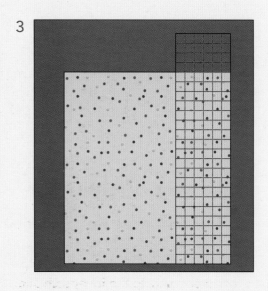

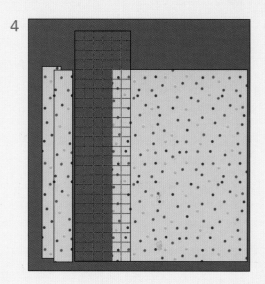

SEAM ALLOWANCE GUIDELINES

All of the seam allowances for projects in this book (and for most quilts) are ¼". The best way to achieve this is to use a ¼" foot that fits your machine, which you likely will need to purchase separately.

If you don't have a ¼" foot, try this method to get accurate seam allowances:

1. Run a piece of tape on your sewing machine ¼" from the needle.

2. Stitch a pair of 2" squares together using a ¼" seam.

3. Measure the seam allowance to see if it is actually ¼".

4. Press the seam open and measure the finished unit. It should measure 3½". If it is less than 3½", make your seam allowance slightly narrower. If it is more than 3½", make your seam allowance slightly wider.

PRESSING BASICS

Pressing can be as important as piecing when it comes to accurately assembling your quilt.

Check iron settings before you begin pressing. Heat and steam can distort pieces.

Remember the difference between ironing and pressing. When you iron fabric, you use the back-and-forth motion of the iron to remove wrinkles. When you press fabric, you lift the iron up and down off the ironing board to avoid shifting pieces or distorting fabric. The techniques can yield different results.

Pressing Seams in a Rotation

This is a great technique that really helps the seams to lay flat. These sample instructions are for a four-patch unit, but this method can be used in other cases, too. Use some scraps to practice this technique.

1. Stitch two squares together. Press the seam to one side.

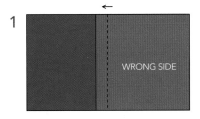

2. Stitch two more squares together. Press the seams to the other side.

3. Lay the segments created in Steps 1 and 2 with right sides together. Because the seams have been pressed in opposite directions, they will interlock and fit together smoothly. Stitch the segments together ¼" from one long edge.

4. Gently release a few stitches on the back in the first seam, then open up the four-patch unit.

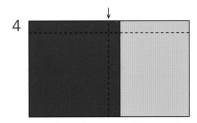

5. Press seams so they all rotate in the same direction, either clockwise or counterclockwise.

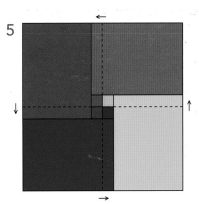

11

APPLIQUÉ BASICS

The appliqué projects in this book were created using Lite Steam-A-Seam 2, a wonderful, slightly tacky paper-backed fusible web. Because it is tacky on both sides, it can be repositioned easily. This fusible web won't gum up your sewing machine needle, and it can't be over-ironed like some fusibles can.

1. Trace the already reversed designs onto one paper side of the fusible web. Remove the paper from the other side.

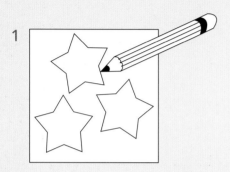

2. Fuse the web to the wrong side of appliqué fabric.

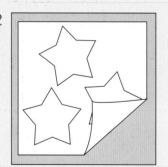

3. Cut out each appliqué on the traced lines.

4. Position each appliqué piece on the background fabric. Fuse each appliqué in place according to the manufacturer's instructions.

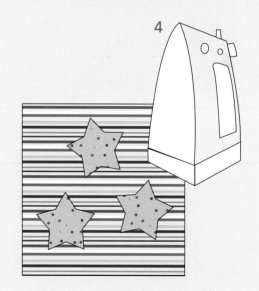

BINDING AND MITERING BASICS

These steps will help you get a perfectly finished border every time.

1. Measure around the edges of the quilt. Piece together a 2¼"-wide strip from the binding fabric that measures the sum of the quilt edges' lengths plus 12".

2. Turn one short end of the binding strip under by ¼" toward the wrong side of the fabric. Press.

3. Fold the binding strip in half lengthwise, with wrong sides together.

4. Lay the folded binding strip on the right side of the quilt in the middle of a side. Make sure the raw edges are even. Begin stitching about 2" from the folded-under end using a ¼" seam allowance.

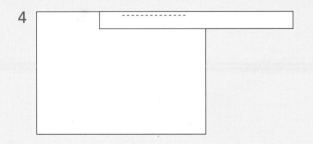

5. Stop stitching ¼" from the corner. Backstitch and clip the threads. Remove the quilt from the sewing machine. Fold the binding strip up and away from the corner of the quilt to form a 45-degree angle in the binding strip.

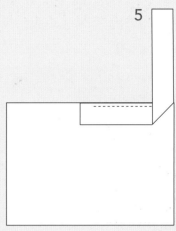

6. Fold the binding strip back down on itself. Begin stitching at the upper edge. Stitch all the way around the quilt, and miter all four corners this way.

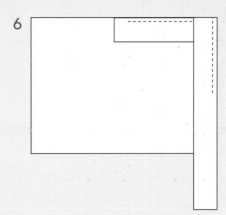

7. Finish the binding by trimming the final edge at an angle so it will tuck inside the beginning of the binding at least 1".

8. Stitch the binding in place, overlapping the original stitching.

9. Press the binding around to the back, and hand stitch it in place.

CHAPTER 2

Stitch a Stunning Sun Porch

A light, cheerful sun porch is the perfect place to unwind after a long day. Quilts and projects can be created in a delightfully sunny array of pale yellow, light and dark rose and vintage blue-greens. A cool drink and your favorite magazine are all that you need to complete the picture. Sit back and relax!

Sunny Throw Quilt

This delightful little quilt was so much fun to make. I love the colors. They remind me of my grandmother's house and all of her beautiful things. **Finished quilt size: 60" x 72". Finished block size: 6" x 6".**

MATERIALS NEEDED

5 light pink fat quarters (block 1)

5 sky blue fat quarters (block 1)

5 rose fat quarters (block 2)

5 yellow fat quarters (block 2)

1 yellow fat quarter (corner blocks)

1 sky blue fat quarter (corner blocks)

1 yd. sky blue (borders)

¾ yd. yellow (borders)

1⅛ yd. rose (border, binding)

4 yd. fabric (backing)

Twin-size batting

Thread

General sewing tools and supplies

FABRIC	CUT	TO YIELD	FOR
Each of 5 pink fat quarters	4 strips, 3⅞" x 18"; cut each into 4 squares, 3⅞" x 3⅞"; cut each into 2 triangles, on the diagonal	160 triangles	Block 1
Each of 5 sky blue fat quarters	4 strips, 3⅞" x 18"; cut each into 4 squares, 3⅞" x 3⅞"; cut each into 2 triangles, on the diagonal	160 triangles	Block 1
Each of 5 rose fat quarters	2 strips, 6⅞" x 18"; cut each into 2 squares, 6⅞" x 6⅞"; cut each into 2 triangles, on the diagonal	40 triangles	Block 2
Each of 5 yellow fat quarters	2 strips, 6⅞" x 18"; cut each into 2 squares, 6⅞" x 6⅞" cut each into 2 triangles, on the diagonal	40 triangles	Block 2
1 yellow fat quarter	2 strips, 3⅞" x 18 cut each into 4 squares, 3⅞" x 3⅞"; cut each into 2 triangles, on the diagonal	16 triangles	Corner block
1 sky blue fat quarter	2 strips, 3⅞" x 18"; cut each into 4 squares, 3⅞" x 3⅞"; cut each into 2 triangles, on the diagonal	16 triangles	Corner block
Yellow fabric	16 selvage-to-selvage strips, 1½" wide	16 strips	Borders
Sky blue fabric	8 selvage-to-selvage strips, 3½" wide	8 strips	Borders
Rose fabric	8 selvage-to-selvage strips, 1½" wide 8 selvage-to-selvage strips, 2¼" wide	8 strips 8 strips	Borders Binding

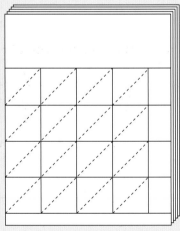
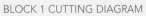

BLOCK 1 CUTTING DIAGRAM

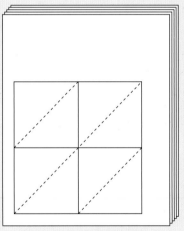

BLOCK 2 CUTTING DIAGRAM

Layer and cut through all of the fat quarters in a group at once to save cutting time. For instance, stack the pink fat quarters, and cut through all of the layers at once. Leave the layers stacked, and cut the squares in half on the diagonal.

Block 1

1. Divide the pink 3⅞" triangles into matching groups of four. Divide the sky blue 3⅞" triangles into matching groups of four. You will have 40 piles of triangles in each color.

2. Match a pink triangle with a blue triangle to create a pink and blue pair. Repeat to match up all of the triangles in each set.

3. Stitch a pink triangle to a blue triangle along the diagonal edge to form a half-square triangle unit. Repeat for all of the pink and blue triangles.

4. Press each unit's seams toward the blue triangles. Repeat for all of the pink and blue sets.

5. Stitch one half-square triangle unit to another to create a two-unit piece. Repeat for all of the half-square triangle units.

6. Press the seams of half of the two-unit pieces to one side, and press the seams of the other half of the units in the opposite direction.

7. Stitch the top unit to the bottom unit to yield an eight-triangle square. Press the seam in rotation. See Chapter 1 for detailed instructions.

    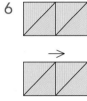 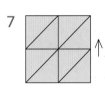 

Block 2

1. Match a rose 6⅞" triangle with a yellow 6⅞" triangle to create 40 yellow and rose pairs.

2. Stitch the rose triangle to the yellow triangle on the diagonal edge to form a half-square triangle unit. Repeat for all of the rose and yellow triangle pairs.

3. Press the seam toward the rose triangle. Repeat for each unit.

Corner Blocks

1. Stitch one yellow triangle to one sky blue triangle ¼" from the diagonal edge to form a half-square triangle unit. Repeat for the remaining yellow and sky blue triangles.

2. Press the seam toward the blue triangle.

3. Stitch one half-square triangle unit to another. Press the seam to one side. Repeat, but press the seam from the second unit in the opposite direction. Repeat this step for each corner block.

4. Stitch the top unit to the bottom unit. Press the seams in rotation. Repeat to create four units.

    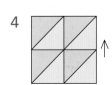

Quilt Top

1. Refer to the Sunny Throw Quilt Layout Diagram. Rotate and place the blocks as needed to create the pattern illustrated. Sew the blocks into 10 rows of eight blocks each. Press all of the seams toward Block 2.

2. Join the rows together. Refer to the Layout Diagram.

Borders

1. Measure the width and length of the quilt.

2. Cut and piece four yellow and two rose border strips that are 1½" x quilt length.

3. Cut and piece two sky blue border strips that are 3½" x quilt length.

4. Stitch the border strips together lengthwise in this order: sky blue, yellow, rose and yellow. Press all seams toward the sky blue strip. Repeat for the remaining border strips.

5. Stitch the borders to either side of the quilt center. Press to the outside.

6. Repeat for the top and bottom borders, except the strips will measure the width of the quilt.

7. Stitch a cornerstone block as shown in Step 8 to either end. Press to the middle.

8. Stitch the borders to the top and bottom of the quilt. Press to the outside.

5

8

FINISH

1. Layer the quilt top, batting and backing.
2. Quilt the piece as desired.

3. Bind the quilt with a narrow rose binding. See Chapter 1 for detailed instructions.

SUNNY THROW QUILT LAYOUT DIAGRAM

Hanging Baskets Wall Quilt

Warm up your garden room or sun room with the pretty palette of colors in this wall quilt. Or, experiment with your own fabric choices to find the look that suits your style and décor. **Finished quilt size: 32" x 32". Finished block size: 11¼" x 11¼".**

MATERIALS NEEDED

2 pink fat quarters (blocks)

2 yellow fat quarters (blocks)

2 rose fat quarters (blocks)

2 blue-green fat quarters (blocks)

1 pink fat quarter (setting squares, cornerstones)

1 green fat quarter (setting squares, cornerstones)

⅓ yd. yellow (borders and sashing)

½ yd. rose (borders, sashing)

⅓ yard blue-green (binding)

1 yd. print (backing)

1 yd. batting

Thread

General sewing tools and supplies

FABRIC	CUT	TO YIELD	FOR
Each of 2 pink fat quarters	4 squares, 2⅞" x 2⅞", cut again on the diagonal	16 triangles	Blocks
	2 rectangles, 2½" x 4½"	4 rectangles	Blocks
	1 square, 4⅞" x 4⅞", cut again on the diagonal	4 triangles; discard 2	Blocks
	4 squares, 3" x 3"	8 squares	Blocks
Each of 2 yellow fat quarters	4 squares, 2⅞" x 2⅞", cut again on the diagonal	16 triangles	Blocks
	2 rectangles, 2½" x 4½"	4 rectangles	Blocks
	1 square, 4⅞" x 4⅞", cut again on the diagonal	4 triangles; discard 2	Blocks
	4 squares, 3" x 3"	8 squares	Blocks
Each of 2 rose fat quarters	4 squares, 2⅞" x 2⅞", cut again on the diagonal	16 triangles	Blocks
	1 square, 4⅞" x 4⅞", cut again on the diagonal	4 triangles; discard 2	Blocks
	1 square, 9¼" x 9¼", cut twice on the diagonal	8 triangles	Blocks
	4 squares, 3" x 3"	8 squares	Blocks
Each of 2 blue-green fat quarters	4 squares, 2⅞" x 2⅞", cut again on the diagonal	16 triangles	Blocks
	1 square, 4⅞" x 4⅞", cut again on the diagonal	4 triangles; discard 2	Blocks
	1 square, 9¼" x 9¼", cut twice on the diagonal	8 triangles	Blocks
	4 squares, 3" x 3"	8 squares	Blocks
Yellow print	4 strips, 1½" x 42"	4 strips	Lattice strips
1 green fat quarter	9 squares, 1½" x 1½"	9 squares	Lattice squares
Rose print	4 strips, 3½" x 42"	4 strips	Borders
1 pink fat quarter	4 squares, 3½" x 3½"	4 squares	Borders

STITCH

Yellow and Rose Blocks

Note: These instructions are for one block. Repeat the steps to make a second identical block.

1. Stitch one yellow 2⅞" triangle to one rose 2⅞" triangle on the diagonal to form a yellow-rose square. Repeat to yield six squares. Press the seams toward the rose triangles.

2. Join three half-square triangle units together in a row. Press the seams to the left.

3. Join two half-square triangle units together. Stitch a 2⅞" yellow triangle to the left side. Press everything to the right.

4. Stitch another yellow triangle to the left side of the final half-square triangle unit. Press the seams to the left.

1

2

3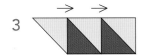

4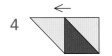

5. Join the three units as shown. Press the seams open.

6. Stitch one 4⅞" rose triangle to the bottom of the unit.

7. Stitch one rose 2⅞" triangle to the right of one 2½" x 4½" yellow rectangle. Stitch one rose triangle to the left of the one yellow rectangle. Press the seams toward the triangles.

8. Stitch one rectangle unit to each of the bottom two sides of the block center. Press the seams toward the rectangle units.

9. Stitch one 4⅞" yellow triangle to the bottom of this unit. Press toward the triangle.

10. Draw a diagonal line from corner to corner on the wrong side of four 3" pink squares; use two squares from one pink fat quarter and two from the other. Lay one 3" square right sides together on the outside corner of each of four large blue-green triangles. Stitch the pieces together on the diagonal line.

11. Trim the extra fabric on each piece to ¼" from the seam.

12. Press the seam on each piece to the outside.

13. Stitch one large, blue-green triangle unit to each side of the center block. Make sure that the same pink corner triangles are opposite each other. Press the seams to the outside. Repeat for the other two sides.

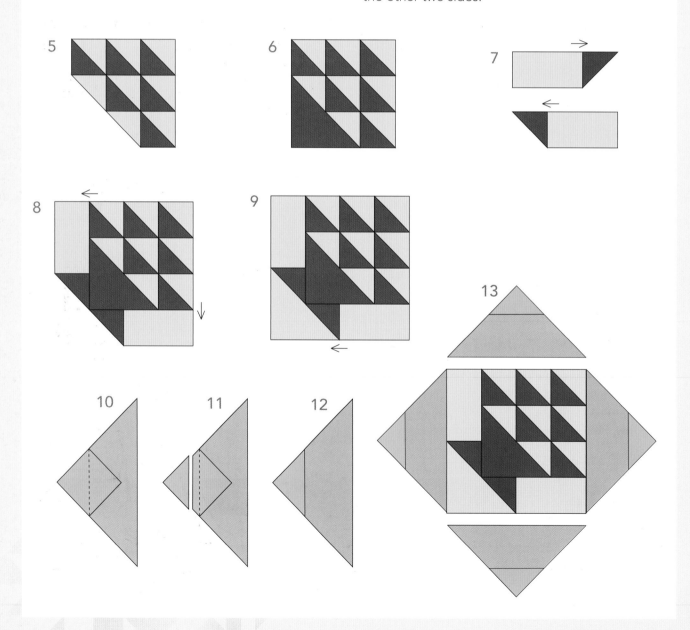

Pink and Blue-Green Blocks

Note: The instructions are for one block. Repeat the steps to make a second identical block.

1. Stitch one pink 2⅞" triangle to one blue-green 2⅞" triangle on the diagonal. Repeat to yield six squares. Press the seams toward the blue-green triangles.

2. Join three half-square triangle units together in a row. Press the seams to the left.

3. Join two half-square triangle units together. Stitch one 2⅞" pink triangle to the left side, and press everything to the right.

4. Stitch another pink triangle to the left side of the final half-square triangle unit. Press to the left.

5. Join the three units from Steps 1 through 4. Press the seams open.

6. Stitch one 4⅞" blue-green triangle to the bottom of this unit.

7. Stitch one blue-green 2⅞" triangle to the right of one 2½" x 4½" pink rectangle and another blue-green triangle to the left of the other pink rectangle. Press toward the triangles.

8. Stitch one rectangle unit to each of the bottom two sides of the block center. Press toward the rectangle units.

9. Stitch one 4⅞" pink triangle to the bottom of this unit. Press toward the triangle.

10. Draw a diagonal line from corner to corner on the wrong side of four of the 3" yellow squares. Use two from one yellow fat quarter and two from the other. Lay one 3" square on the outside corner of each of four large rose triangles. Stitch the pieces together on the diagonal.

11. Trim the extra fabric on each piece to ¼" from the seam.

12. Press the seam on each piece to the outside.

13. Stitch a large rose triangle unit to either side of the center block. Make sure that the same yellow corner triangles are opposite each other. Press the seams to the outside. Repeat for the other two sides.

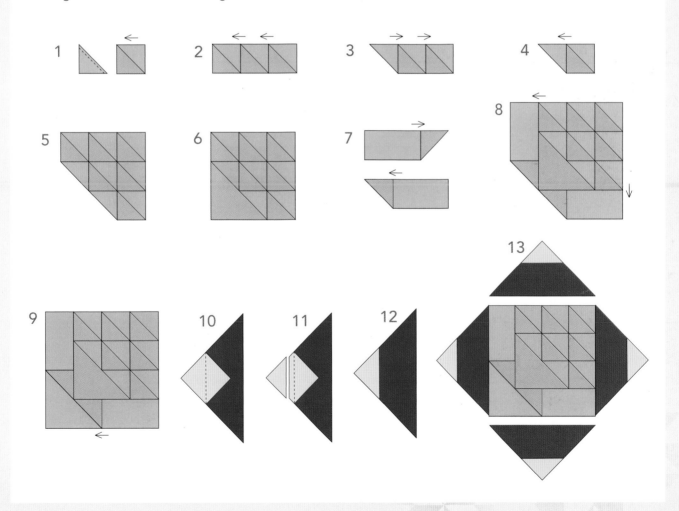

Quilt Top

1. Measure the blocks. Cut the lattice strips into 12 lengths that are 1½" x the block size.

2. Sew together three lattice strips and two blocks in an alternating pattern, beginning with a lattice strip. Repeat. Refer to the Hanging Baskets Wall Quilt Layout Diagram.

3. Sew together three 1½" green squares and two lattice strips end to end in an alternating pattern, beginning with a green square. Repeat two more times.

4. Sew together the three lattice strips and two block rows in an alternating pattern, beginning with the lattice strips.

HANGING BASKETS WALL QUILT LAYOUT DIAGRAM

Borders

1. Measure the quilt top. Trim the 3½"-wide rose strips to fit.

2. Stitch one border strip to each side of the quilt top. Press the seams to the outside.

3. Stitch one 3½" pink square to each end of the two remaining border strips. Press the seams away from the squares.

4. Stitch one border strip with squares to the top and bottom of the quilt top. Press the seams to the outside.

FINISH

1. Layer the quilt top, batting and backing.
2. Quilt the piece as desired.

3. Bind the quilt with a narrow blue-green binding. See Chapter 1 for detailed instructions.

Super Simple Fat Quarter Pillows

It's never been so easy to spruce up a room. These quick and easy pillows go together in a flash, and four fat quarters will yield two pillows. Mix and match the triangle sets, or stitch both pillows the same. It's all up to you. **Finished pillow size: 16" x 16".**

MATERIALS NEEDED

(For two pillows)

1 pink fat quarter (pillow)

1 yellow fat quarter (pillow)

1 rose fat quarter (pillow)

1 blue-green fat quarter (pillow)

2 yd. fabric (lining)

2 yd. batting

2 bags fiberfill

4 covered buttons, 1¼" in diameter (covered buttons)

Fabric scraps (covered buttons)

Long sewing needle

Heavy thread

Thread

General sewing tools and supplies

FABRIC	CUT	TO YIELD	FOR
Pink fat quarter	1 square, 17¼" x 17¼"; cut again on the diagonal twice	4 triangles	Pillow blocks
Yellow fat quarter	1 square, 17¼" x 17¼"; cut again on the diagonal twice	4 triangles	Pillow blocks
Rose fat quarter	1 square, 17¼" x 17¼"; cut again on the diagonal twice	4 triangles	Pillow blocks
Blue-green fat quarter	1 square, 17¼" x 17¼"; cut again on the diagonal twice	4 triangles	Pillow blocks

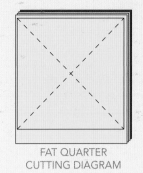

FAT QUARTER
CUTTING DIAGRAM

**Note: Layer all four fat quarters and cut them at once.

STITCH

1. Stitch the triangles together in pairs, and press the seams open. Make four of each color pair.

2. Stitch two paired triangles together to form a square. Press the seams open again.

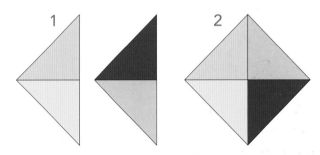

FINISH

1. Layer the finished squares, batting and backing.

2. Quilt the pieces as desired.

3. Lay two quilted squares right sides together. Stitch ¼" from the edge all the way around, leaving an opening on one side for stuffing. Repeat for the other pillow.

4. Turn the pillow right side out; stuff it with fiberfill. Slipstitch the opening shut.

5. Cover the buttons with scrap fabrics; follow the manufacturer's directions.

6. Center a button on each side of the pillow. Use the long sewing needle and heavy thread to stitch from button to button through the middle of the pillow; pull up the threads to make the center of the pillow dip in. Repeat for the other pillow. Refer to the Super Simple Fat Quarter Pillows Layout Diagram.

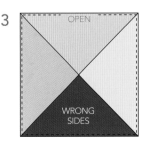

SUPER SIMPLE FAT QUARTER PILLOWS LAYOUT DIAGRAM

CHAPTER 3

Sew a Sensational Kitchen

Create a fun, bright kitchen that is just the right mix of past and present. From appliquéd cloth napkins that add a touch of casual elegance to the coordinating place mats, table runner, tea towels and kitchen quilt, these projects will bring a cheery touch to the busiest room in the home.

Kitchen Crossings Quilt

Brighten up your kitchen table with this delightful little quilt, or take it with you for a sunny summer picnic. **Finished quilt size: 61" x 61". Finished block size: 7½" x 7½".**

MATERIALS NEEDED

4 yellow fat quarters (blue block, red block)

2 blue fat quarters (blue block)

2 green fat quarters (green block)

2 red fat quarters (red block)

½ yd. yellow (print block)

1½ yd. light blue print (print block)

2½ yd. stripe (blocks, wide border)

½ yd. red (narrow border)

⅛ yd. yellow (cornerstones)

¾ yd. green (binding)

4 yd. print (backing)

Twin-size batting

Thread

General sewing tools and supplies

FABRIC	CUT	TO YIELD	FOR
Light blue print	24 squares, 8" x 8"	24 squares	Print block
½ yd. yellow	96 squares, 2" x 2"	96 squares	Print block
Stripe	13 strips, 2" x 40"; then cut each strip again into 8 strips, 2" x 5"	104 strips (discard 4)	Green, Blue and Red blocks
Yellow fat quarters	4 strips, 2" x 20"	4 strips	Blue block
	36 squares, 2" x 2"	36 squares	Blue block
	4 strips, 2" x 20"	4 strips	Red block
	32 squares, 2" x 2"	32 squares	Red block
	4 strips, 2" x 20"	4 strips	Green block
	32 squares, 2" x 2"	32 squares	Green block
	4 squares, 3½" x 3½"	4 squares	Cornerstones
Blue fat quarters	5 strips, 2" x 20"	5 strips	Blue block
	72 squares, 2" x 2"	72 squares	Blue block
Red fat quarters	5 strips, 2" x 20"	5 strips	Red block
	64 squares, 2" x 2"	64 squares	Red block
Green fat quarters	5 strips, 2" x 20"	5 strips	Green block
	64 squares, 2" x 2"	64 squares	Green block
½ yd. red	4 strips, 1½" x 3½"	4 strips	Narrow border
	4 strips, 1½" x 4½"	4 strips	Narrow border

STITCH

Print Block

1. Draw a corner-to-corner diagonal line on the wrong side of each of the 96 yellow 2" squares.

2. Lay a 2" yellow square right sides together on each corner of an 8" light blue square. Stitch the squares together on the diagonal lines.

3. Trim the extra layers of fabric to ¼".

4. Press the seams to the outside. Repeat for the other 23 blocks.

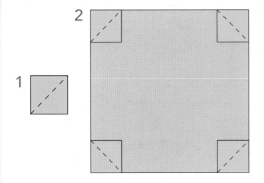

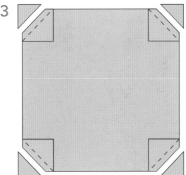

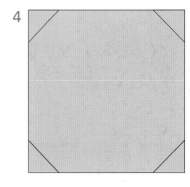

Cut all of the pieces for one block type at once, and keep everything together in a group that is to be sewn together.

Blue, Red and Green Blocks

Note: The blue block will be used for the illustrations. Repeat the instructions for the red and green blocks. You will make nine blue, eight red and eight green blocks.

1. Stitch one blue strip, one yellow strip and another blue strip together in that order. Press the seams toward the blue strips. Repeat. Cut each strip set into nine 2" segments to yield a total of 18 segments. For the red and green blocks, you will need only 16 segments.

2. Stitch one yellow strip, one blue strip and another yellow strip together in that order. Press the seams toward the blue strip. Cut this strip set into nine 2" segments to yield a total of nine segments. For the red and green blocks, you will need only eight segments.

3. Position one segment from Step 1 on each side of one segment from Step 2.

4. Stitch the segments together to make a nine-patch unit. Make nine blue units, eight red units and eight green units. Press the seams to the outside.

5. Draw a corner-to-corner diagonal line on the wrong side of each of the remaining 2" blue squares.

6. With right sides together, lay a 2" blue square on either end of a 2" x 5" striped rectangle. Stitch the pieces together on the diagonal lines.

7. Trim the extra layers of fabric to ¼".

8. Press the seams toward the outside.

9. Stitch one of the striped units to each side of the nine-patch center. Press to the outside.

10. Stitch one 2" yellow square to each side of the remaining striped units. Press the seams to the center.

11. Sew one remaining striped unit to the top and bottom of each nine-patch unit. Press the seams to the outside.

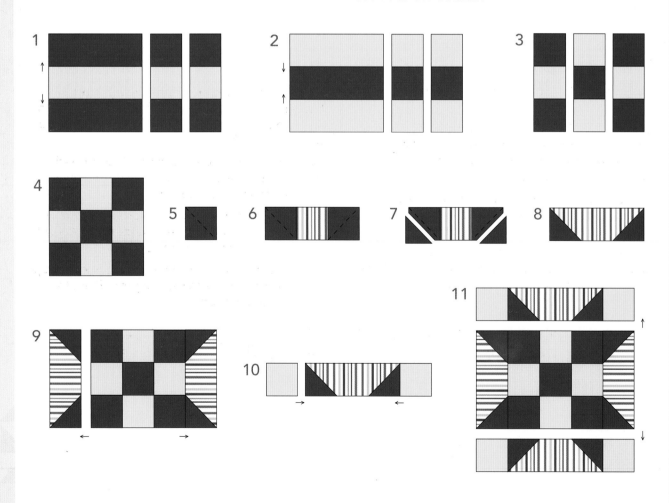

Quilt Top

1. Stitch the blocks into rows; refer to the Kitchen Crossings Quilt Layout Diagram. Press the seams toward the print blocks.

2. Join the rows together; refer to the Kitchen Crossings Quilt Layout Diagram. Press the rows open so that the seams will lay flat.

Cornerstones

1. Stitch one 1½" x 3½" red strip to one side of each 3½" yellow square. Press the seams toward the red strip.

2. Stitch one 1½" x 4½" red strip to the adjacent side of each yellow square. Press the seams toward the red strip.

Borders

1. Measure the length and width of the quilt center.

2. Cut and piece together two narrow red borders that measure 1½" wide x the quilt top's length, and two striped borders that measure 3½" wide x the quilt top's length.

3. Stitch one red border strip to each striped border strip. Press the seams toward the red border. These are the side borders.

4. With the red border to the inside, stitch one border unit on each side of the quilt center. Refer to the Kitchen Crossings Quilt Layout Diagram.

5. Cut and piece together two narrow red borders that measure 1½" x the quilt top's width and two striped borders that measure 3½" x the quilt top's width.

6. Stitch one red border strip to each striped border strip. Press the seams toward the red border. These are the top and bottom borders.

7. Stitch one cornerstone block to each end of the top and bottom borders. Refer to the Layout Diagram. Press the seams to the inside.

8. With the red border to the inside, add the top and bottom borders to the quilt top. Press the seams to the outside.

FINISH

1. Layer the quilt top, batting and backing.
2. Quilt the piece as desired.

3. Bind the quilt with a narrow green binding. See Chapter 1 for detailed instructions.

KITCHEN CROSSINGS QUILT LAYOUT DIAGRAM

My Cup of Tea Table Runner

This delightful project is perfect to grace your kitchen table or wall. Sit down and enjoy a cup of tea with this happy little quilt. **Finished runner size: 20" x 40".**

MATERIALS NEEDED

1 blue fat quarter (appliqués, outer border)

1 red fat quarter (appliqués, outer border)

1 yellow fat quarter (appliqués, outer border)

1 green fat quarter (appliqués, outer border)

½ yd. white print (background blocks)

½ yd. yellow print (inner border)

Scraps of blue, red, yellow and green (appliqués)

½ yd. stripe (binding)

¾ yd. fabric of your choice (backing)

Craft-size batting

Paper-backed fusible web (appliqué)

Yellow 40-weight embroidery thread* (appliqué)

Appliqué patterns from the back of the book: Teapot, Teacup, Large Flower

Thread

General sewing tools and supplies

*SULKY 40-WEIGHT EMBROIDERY THREAD NO. 1024 WAS USED FOR THE PROJECT SHOWN.

FABRIC	CUT	TO YIELD	FOR
Blue, red, yellow and green fat quarters	Layer all four fat quarters; cut 3 strips, 2½" x 18"	12 strips	Outer border
White print	4 squares, 8½" x 8½"	4 squares	Background blocks
Yellow print	2 strips, 3½" x 33½"	2 strips	Inner border
	2 strips, 2½" x 16½"	2 strips	Inner border

STITCH

Strip Sets and Background Blocks

1. Stitch one set of strips from the fat quarters together as shown in this order: blue, red, green and yellow. Repeat to make three strip sets. Press all of the seams to one side.

2. Cut each strip set into six segments, each 2½" wide, to yield a total of 18 segments.

3. Stitch two segments end to end to create the top border. Repeat for the bottom border. Press all of the squares to one side in the same direction.

4. Stitch five segments together to create one side border. Repeat for the other side border. Press all of the squares to one side in the same direction.

5. Stitch one segment to the right side of each of two white print 8½" squares. Press away from the white squares.

6. Stitch one segment to the left side of each of two white print 8½" squares. Press away from the white squares.

7. Stitch all four white print squares together as shown, alternating the placement of the colored block strips. Press the seams open on the white background block.

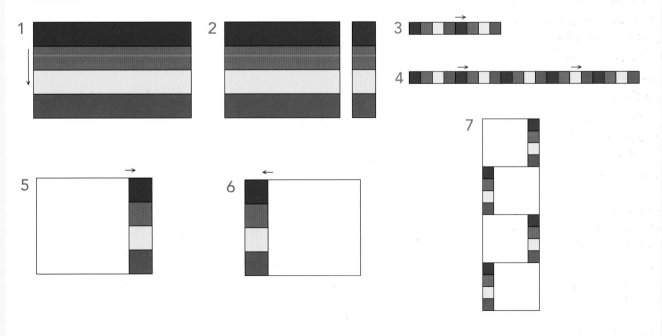

Borders

1. Stitch one yellow 3½" x 32½" border to each side of the background block. Press the seams to the outside.

2. Stitch one yellow 2½" x 16½" border to the top and bottom of the background block. Press the seams to the outside.

3. Stitch one short strip set each to the top and bottom as shown. Stitch one longer strip set to each side as shown.

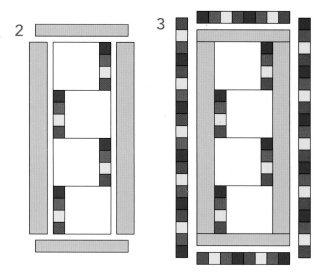

APPLIQUÉ

Note: See Chapter 1 for detailed instructions on fusible appliqué.

1. On the wrong side of the fusible web, trace the parts for one Teapot, three Teacups and three Large Flowers. The designs already have been reversed.

2. Iron the fusible web to the wrong side of the coordinating fabric scraps. Cut out the pieces on the traced lines.

3. Refer to the My Cup of Tea Table Runner Layout Diagram to position the appliqué pieces on the wall hanging. Press the appliqué pieces in place; follow the manufacturer's directions.

4. Zigzag stitch around the edges of the appliqués using yellow embroidery thread.

FINISH

1. Layer the quilt top, batting and backing.

2. Quilt the piece as desired.

3. Bind the quilt with a narrow binding of the striped fabric. See Chapter 1 for detailed instructions.

MY CUP OF TEA TABLE RUNNER LAYOUT DIAGRAM

Neat Little Napkins

These quick and easy napkins take only one fat quarter each, plus a few scraps. What a great way to add some elegance to your mealtimes! **Finished napkin size: 16" x 16".**

MATERIALS NEEDED

(For four napkins)

1 red fat quarter (napkin)

1 blue fat quarter (napkin)

1 green fat quarter (napkin)

1 yellow fat quarter (napkin)

⅛ yd. white print (napkin)

Scraps of red, blue, green and yellow (appliqués)

40-weight embroidery thread in yellow, green, red and blue*

Paper-backed fusible web

General sewing tools and supplies

Appliqué pattern from the back of the book: Small Flower

* SULKY 40-WEIGHT EMBROIDERY THREADS NO. 1037, NO. 1024, NO. 1196 AND NO. 1510 WERE USED FOR THE PROJECT SHOWN.

FABRIC	CUT	TO YIELD	FOR
Red, Blue, Green and Yellow fat quarters	Layer all of the fat quarters; cut 1 square, 16½" x 16½", from each	4 squares	Napkins
White print	4 squares, 3½" x 3½"	4 squares	Background squares

STITCH

1. Turn under ¼" of the top and bottom edges of one 16½" napkin square. Press. Turn under ¼" of each of the square's side edges. Press. Repeat to turn under a total of ½" on each side of the napkin square. Press. Repeat this step for each napkin square.

2. Zigzag stitch each napkin ¼" from the edge on the right side to catch the fold in the back.

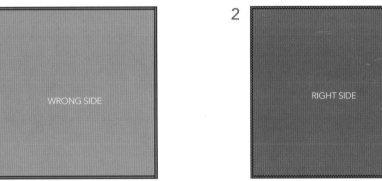

APPLIQUÉ

Note: See Chapter 1 for detailed instructions on fusible appliqué.

1. On the wrong side of the fusible web, trace the parts for four Small Flowers. Remember, the designs already have been reversed.

2. Iron the fusible web pieces to the wrong side of the coordinating fabric scraps. Cut out the appliqué pieces on the traced lines.

3. Iron fusible web to the wrong side of each of the 3½" white background squares.

4. Position one 3½" square on the diagonal on one of the napkins, 4" from one of the corners. Place one flower and one flower center on top of the background square; mix up the flower and flower center colors as shown in the Neat Little Napkins Layout Diagrams or as desired. Iron the flower and flower center appliqué pieces in place. Repeat for the remaining napkins.

5. Use a contrasting thread to zigzag stitch around the appliquéd flower, flower center and background square. Refer to the Neat Little Napkins Layout Diagrams. Repeat for the remaining napkins.

Dynamite Dish Towels

Create these adorable dish towels to coordinate with all of the other kitchen projects. What a fantastic way to use up your scraps and liven up doing the dishes!
Finished towel size: Depends on towel size used.
Finished block size: 6½" x 6½".

MATERIALS NEEDED

(For three towels)

3 dish towels, 20" x 28" in yellow, blue and green

1 white print fat quarter (background squares)

Scraps of red, yellow, blue and green (appliqués)

3 buttons, one each in red, yellow and blue (flower centers)

Paper-backed fusible web

Thread

40-weight embroidery thread in blue, green and red*

Appliqué patterns from the back of the book: Teacup, Small Flower

General sewing tools and supplies

SULKY 40-WEIGHT EMBROIDERY THREADS NO. 1037, 1196 AND 1510 WERE USED FOR THE PROJECT SHOWN.

FABRIC	CUT	TO YIELD	FOR
White print	3 squares, 6½" x 6½"	3 squares	Background squares
Red scraps	2 squares, 1½" x 1½", cut again on the diagonal	4 triangles	Corner triangles
Yellow scraps	2 squares, 1½" x 1½", cut again on the diagonal	4 triangles	Corner triangles
Green scraps	2 squares, 1½" x 1½", cut again on the diagonal	4 triangles	Corner triangles

APPLIQUÉ

Note: See Chapter 1 for detailed instructions on fusible appliqué.

1. Iron fusible web to the wrong side of one white background square. Position the square in the center of one dish towel, 2" from the bottom. Fuse the square in place. Repeat for the remaining background squares.

2. Iron fusible web to the wrong side of one set of corner triangles. Place the triangles on the corners of one white square, and fuse in place as shown. Match the corner triangle colors to the dish towels as shown in the Dynamite Dish Towels Layout Diagrams, or make your own color scheme as desired. For each towel, I used the same colors for the center of the cup and the corner triangles, and I matched the flower with the color of the towel.

3. On the wrong side of fusible web, trace the parts for three Teacups and three Small Flowers. Remember, the designs already have been reversed.

4. Iron the fusible web to the wrong side of the coordinating fabric scraps. Cut out the pieces on the traced lines.

5. Position one teacup and one flower on each white background square, matching the colors and parts as shown in the Layout Diagram. Fuse the flower and teacup pieces into place.

6. Zigzag stitch around the edges of the appliqué pieces; use a contrasting embroidery thread as shown.

7. Stitch a button to the center of the flower. You can match the colors as shown, or choose your own color scheme.

8. Repeat Steps 5 through 7 for the remaining dish towels.

2
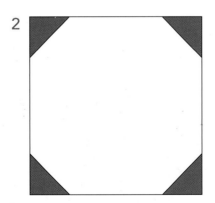

DYNAMITE DISH TOWELS BLOCK LAYOUT DIAGRAMS (FROM LEFT) FOR THE YELLOW TOWEL, BLUE TOWEL AND GREEN TOWEL

Pretty Please Place Mats

With only four coordinating fat quarters and a stripe fabric, you can create four beautiful place mats. Treat your own family, or make an awesome shower gift for that new bride. **Finished place mat size: 12" x 18".**

MATERIALS NEEDED

(For four place mats)

1 red fat quarter

1 yellow fat quarter

1 blue fat quarter

1 green fat quarter

½ yd. stripe (border)

⅝ yd. blue (binding)

1 yd. coordinating fabric (backing)

1 yd. batting

¼ yd. fusible web (appliqués)

Thread

40-weight embroidery thread in red, yellow, blue and green*

Appliqué pattern from the back of the book: Large Flower

General sewing tools and supplies

* SULKY 40-WEIGHT EMBROIDERY THREADS NO. 1037, NO. 1024, NO. 1196 AND NO. 1510 WERE USED FOR THE PROJECT SHOWN.

You can layer all four fat quarters, cut them at once, and then mix and match the pieces to create four different looks. After you cut the pieces, divide them into groups according to the diagrams.

FABRIC	CUT	TO YIELD	FOR
Each fat quarter	Layer the fat quarters. Then cut: • 1 square, 4½" x 4½" • 16 squares, 2½" x 2½" • 8 squares, 2⅞" x 2⅞", cut once on the diagonal • 8 rectangles, 2½" x 4½"	4 squares 64 squares 64 triangles 32 rectangles	A B, D and H F and G C and E
Stripe	8 rectangles, 3½" x 12½"	32 rectangles	Borders

FAT QUARTER CUTTING DIAGRAM

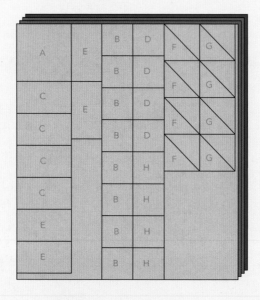

COLOR BLOCK PLACEMENT

MAT	A, H	B, D, F	C, G	E	FLOWER	CENTER
1	Yellow	Red	Blue	Green	Green	Red
2	Red	Green	Yellow	Blue	Blue	Red
3	Green	Blue	Red	Yellow	Yellow	Blue
4	Blue	Yellow	Green	Red	Red	Green

BLOCK LAYOUT DIAGRAM

Note: Stitch all of the center blocks of each place mat at the same time. Refer to the Color Block Placement chart and the Pretty Please Place Mats Layout Diagrams for color placement. Repeat the instructions to create four blocks.

1. Stitch eight 2⅞" Triangle F pieces to eight 2⅞" Triangle G pieces. Press to one side. Make eight FG units per block, and set four units per block aside.

2. Stitch one FG unit to each side of one Rectangle E. Press to the outside. Repeat to make two of FGEGF units per block.

3. Stitch one 2½" Square H to either side of one FGEGF unit. Press to the outside. Repeat to make two HFGEGFH units per block.

4. Draw a diagonal line on the wrong side of eight 2½" Square B pieces. Set aside eight Square B pieces per block.

5. With right sides together, lay one Square B on one end of a 2½" x 4½" Rectangle C. Stitch on the diagonal line.

6. Trim the extra layers of fabric to ¼".

7. Press the seam to the outside.

8. Repeat Steps 5, 6 and 7 for the other end of the rectangle to make a flying geese unit. Repeat Steps 4 through 7 to make four flying geese units per block, but set two units per block aside.

9. Stitch one 2½" Square D to each side of the remaining flying geese units.

10. Press toward the middle. Repeat to make two DBCBD units per block.

11. Stitch one FG unit to each side of one DBCBD unit.

12. Press to the middle. Make two FGDBCBDFG units per block.

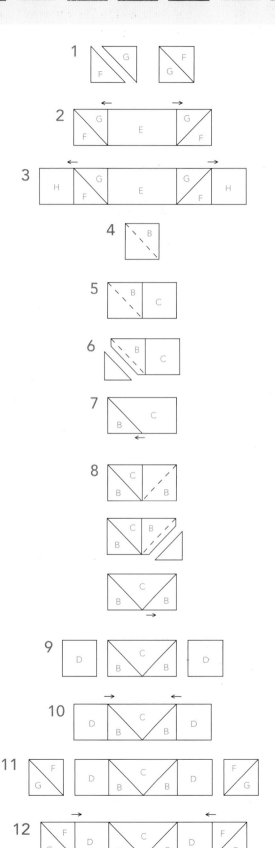

13. Stitch one of the reserved BCB flying geese units to each side of 4½" Square A to create a center block unit. Repeat to make one center block unit per place mat.

14. Press the center block unit to the outside.

15. Stitch one 2½" x 4½" Rectangle E to each side of one center block unit. Repeat for the remaining center block units.

16. Press to the outside.

17. Stitch one GFDBCBDFG unit to the top and bottom of one center block unit. Stitch one HFGEGFH unit to the top and bottom of each center block unit. Repeat for the remaining center block units.

18. Press to the outside.

19. Stitch a 3½" x 12½" striped fabric rectangle to each side of the finished block. Repeat for the remaining place mats.

20. Press to the outside.

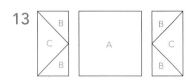

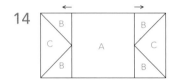

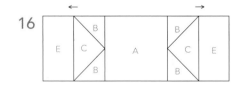

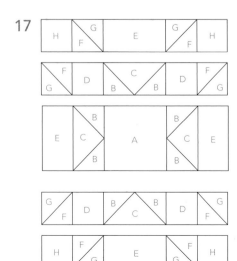

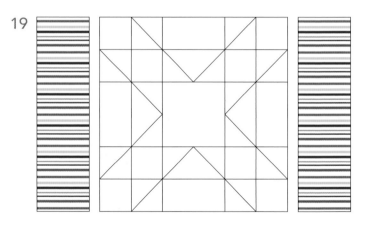

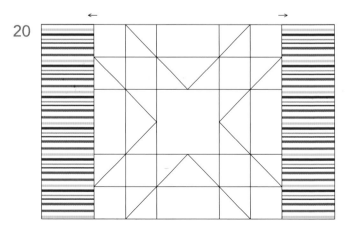

APPLIQUÉ

Note: See Chapter 1 for detailed instructions on fusible appliqué.

1. On the wrong side of the fusible web, trace the parts for four Large Flowers. Remember, the designs already have been reversed.

2. Iron the fusible web to the wrong side of the fabric scraps. Cut out the appliqué pieces on the traced lines.

3. Refer to the Pretty Please Place Mat Layout Diagrams to position one flower on each place mat. Press the appliqués in place; follow the manufacturer's directions.

4. Zigzag stitch around the edges of the appliqué pieces; use a contrasting embroidery thread.

FINISH

1. Layer the place mat top, batting and backing.

2. Quilt the piece as desired.

3. Bind the placemat with a narrow blue binding. See Chapter 1 for detailed instructions.

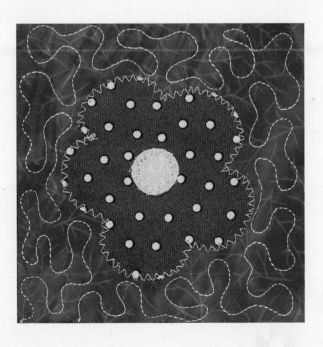

PRETTY PLEASE PLACE MAT 1 LAYOUT DIAGRAM

PRETTY PLEASE PLACE MAT 3 LAYOUT DIAGRAM

PRETTY PLEASE PLACE MAT 2 LAYOUT DIAGRAM

PRETTY PLEASE PLACE MAT 4 LAYOUT DIAGRAM

CHAPTER 4

Design a Delightful Den

These cozy projects in burgundy, hunter green, navy and taupe will make this room your family's retreat of choice on cold winter evenings. Grab the popcorn, then relax together with a favorite movie or your family pictures.

Simply Stripes Quilt

This quilt goes together so easily that it is perfect for that first quilt, or for the quilter who wants to get a project finished in a hurry. Let's get piecing! **Finished quilt size: 61" x 83".**

MATERIALS NEEDED

12 fat quarters in an assortment of colors (stripes)

1 yd. cream (sashing)

1½ yd. multicolored print (border)

¾ yd. burgundy print (binding)

5½ yd. hunter green print (backing)

Full-size batting

Thread

General sewing tools and supplies

FABRIC	CUT	TO YIELD	FOR
Each of 12 fat quarters	5 strips, 3½" x 18"	60 strips	Strip sets

CUTTING DIAGRAM

3½" X 18"

STITCH

Strip Sets

1. Join the strips together lengthwise as shown to create five strip sets with 12 different fabrics in each. Sew the fabrics together in the same order for each set. Press all of the strips in the same direction.

2. From each strip set, cut two widths, each 8½", to yield 10 strip sets.

3. Join two 8½"-wide strip sets end to end; make sure the fabrics in each strip set repeat in the same order. Join the remaining strip sets to yield a total of five long strip sets.

1

2

3

Sashing and Borders

1. From the cream fabric, cut and piece together six sashing strips that measure 2" x 72½" each.

2. Add the sashing strips to the strip sets to make the quilt center. Make sure all of the strip sets are oriented in the same direction; refer to the Simply Stripes Quilt Layout Diagram. Stitch one sashing strip to the left side of the first strip set, then alternate sashing strips and strip sets until the quilt top is assembled as shown in the layout diagram. Press the seams toward the cream strips.

3. From the cream fabric, cut and piece together two sashing strips that measure 2" x 49½" each.

4. Stitch one sashing strip to the top of the quilt center and another to the bottom of the quilt center. Press the seams toward the cream strips.

5. Cut and piece together two borders that measure 6½" x 75½". Stitch one border to each side of the quilt top. Press the seams toward the outside.

6. Cut and piece together two borders that measure 4½" x 61½". Stitch one border to the top and another to the bottom of the quilt top. Press the seams toward the outside.

FINISH

1. Layer the quilt top, batting and backing.

2. Quilt the piece as desired.

3. Bind the quilt. See Chapter 1 for detailed instructions.

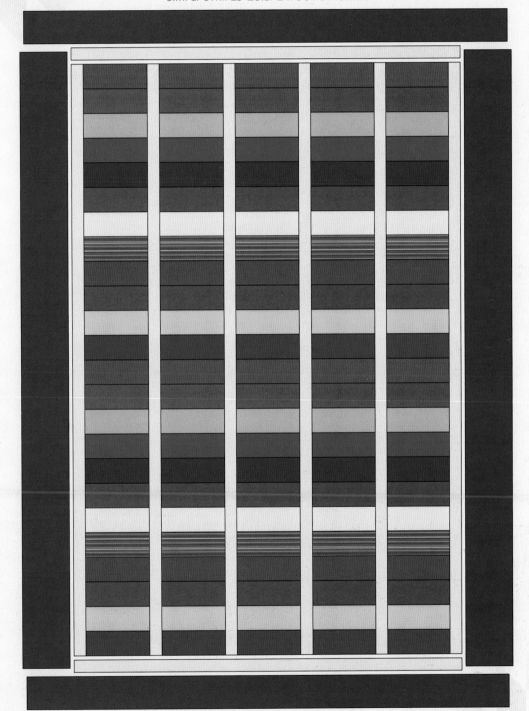

Chickens on the Courthouse Steps Wall Hanging

So many beautiful fabrics out in the quilt shops seem to call my name and beg to be featured as block centers, like this toile print that features colorful chickens. My friend, Debby Sissman, designed the fabric in this wall hanging, and it was so much fun to use. Find fabrics that speak to your creative spirit, and you'll enjoy projects that much more. **Finished quilt size: 50" x 50".**

MATERIALS NEEDED

2 cream fat quarters (blocks 1 and 2)

3 dark green fat quarters (blocks 1 and 2)

1 medium blue fat quarter (block 1)

2 cranberry fat quarters (block 1)

2 green fat quarters (block 1)

1 red fat quarter (block 2)

1 medium blue fat quarter (block 2)

2 dark green fat quarters (block 2)

2 navy fat quarters (block 2)

3 gold fat quarters (sashing)

1 yd. novelty print (center squares)

Scraps of cranberry (cornerstones)

⅝ yd. navy (borders)

½ yd. dark green (binding)

2¾ yd. fabric of your choice (backing)

Craft or twin-size batting

Thread

General sewing tools and supplies

FABRIC	CUT	TO YIELD	FOR
2 cream fat quarters	2 strips, 1½" x 18"; cut each strip again into 8 squares, 1½" x 1½"	16 squares	Sashing
	10 strips, 1½" x 18"	20 strips	Blocks 1 and 2
3 gold fat quarters	3 strips, 14½" x 18"; cut each strip again into 8 strips, 1½" x 14½"	24 strips	Sashing
Novelty print	9 squares, 6½" x 6½"	9 squares	Center squares
Cranberry scraps	4 squares, 2½" x 2½"	4 squares	Cornerstones
3 dark green fat quarters	2 strips, 6½" x 18"; set one strip aside and cut the other into 10 segments, 1½" x 6½" (see cutting diagram)	1 strip 10 segments	Block 1 Block 1
	2 strips, 10½" x 18"; set one strip aside and cut the other into 8 segments, 1½" x 10½"	1 strip 8 segments	Block 2 Block 2
1 medium blue fat quarter	2 strips, 8½" x 18"; set one strip aside and cut the other into 10 segments, 1½" x 8½"	1 strip 10 segments	Block 1 Block 1
2 cranberry fat quarters	2 strips, 10½" x 18"; set one strip aside and cut the other into 10 segments, 1½" x 10½"	1 strip 10 segments	Block 1 Block 1
2 green fat quarters	2 strips, 12½" x 18"; set one strip aside and cut the other into 10 segments, 1½" x 12½"	1 strip 10 segments	Block 1 Block 1
1 red fat quarter	2 strips, 6½" x 18"; set one strip aside and cut the other into 8 segments, 1½" x 6½" (see Cutting Diagram)	1 strip 8 segments	Block 2 Block 2
1 blue fat quarter	2 strips, 8½" x 18"; set one strip aside and cut the other into 8 segments, 1½" x 8½"	1 strip 8 segments	Block 2 Block 2
2 navy fat quarters	2 strips, 12½" x 18"; set one strip aside and cut the other into 8 segments, 1½" x 12½"	1 strip 8 segments	Block 2 Block 2

GREEN FAT QUARTER CUTTING DIAGRAM

RED FAT QUARTER CUTTING DIAGRAM

STITCH

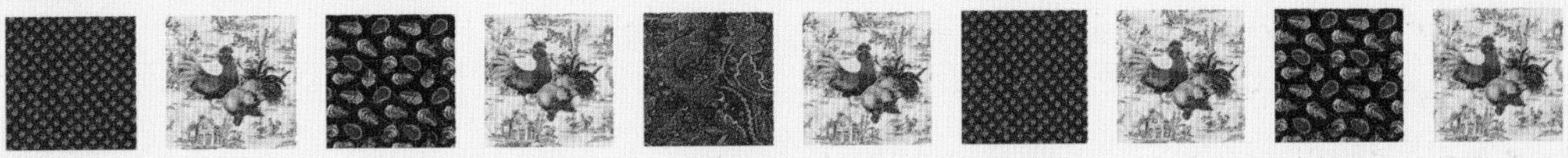

Block 1

Note: The instructions are for one block; repeat the steps to make five blocks.

1. Stitch one cream 1½" x 18" strip to the top and bottom of the dark green 6½" x 18" strip. Press the seams toward the dark green.

2. Cut the cream and dark green strip set into 10 segments, each 1½" x 8½", as shown.

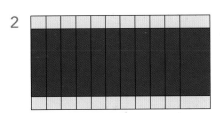

3. Stitch one cream 1½" x 18" strip to the top and bottom of the medium blue 8½" x 18" strip. Press the seams toward the medium blue.

4. Cut the cream and medium blue strip set into 10 units, each 1½" x 10½".

5. Stitch one cream 1½" x 18" strip to the top and bottom of the cranberry 10½" x 18" strip. Press the seams toward the cranberry.

6. Cut the cream and cranberry strip set into 10 units, each 1½" x 12½".

7. Stitch one cream 1½" x 18" strip to the top and bottom of the green 12½" x 18" strip. Press the seams toward the green.

8. Cut the cream and green strip set into 10 units, 1½" x 14½".

9. Stitch one dark green 1½" x 6½" strip to the top and bottom of one 6½" center square; refer to the Block 1 Layout Diagram. Press the seams to the outside.

10. Stitch one dark green and cream segment to each side of the center unit. Press the seams to the outside.

11. Stitch one medium blue 1½" x 8½" strip to the top and bottom of the center unit. Press the seams to the outside.

12. Stitch one medium blue and cream segment to each side of the center unit. Press the seams to the outside.

13. Stitch one cranberry 1½" x 10½" strip to the top and bottom of the center unit. Press the seams to the outside.

14. Stitch one cranberry and cream segment to each side of the center unit. Press the seams to the outside.

15. Stitch one green 1½" x 12½" strip to the top and bottom of the center unit. Press the seams to the outside.

16. Stitch one green and cream segment to each side of the center unit. Press the seams to the outside.

BLOCK 1 LAYOUT DIAGRAM

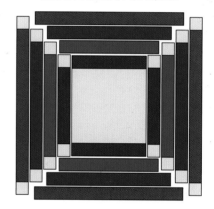

Block 2

Note: The instructions are for one block; repeat the steps to make four blocks.

1. Stitch one cream 1½" x 18" strip to the top and bottom of the red 6½" x 18" strip. Press the seams toward the red.

2. Cut the cream and red strip set into eight segments, each 1½" x 8½", as shown.

3. Stitch one cream 1½" x 18" strip to the top and bottom of the blue 8½" x 18" strip. Press the seams toward the blue.

4. Cut the cream and medium blue strip set into eight units, each 1½" x 10½".

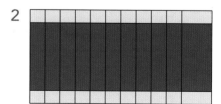

5. Stitch one cream 1½" x 18" strip to the top and bottom of the dark green 10½" x 18" strip. Press the seams toward the dark green.

6. Cut the cream and dark green strip set into eight units, each 1½" x 12½".

7. Stitch one cream 1½" x 18" strip to the top and bottom of the navy 12½" x 18" strip. Press the seams toward the navy.

8. Cut the cream and navy strip set into 10 units, 1½" x 14½".

9. Stitch one red 1½" x 6½" strip to the top and bottom of one 6½" center square; refer to the Block 1 Layout Diagram. Press the seams to the outside.

10. Stitch one red and cream corner segment to each side of the center unit. Press the seams to the outside.

11. Stitch one medium blue 1½" x 8½" strip to the top and bottom of the center unit. Press the seams to the outside.

12. Stitch one medium blue and cream segment to each side of the center unit. Press the seams to the outside.

13. Stitch one dark green 1½" x 10½" strip to the top and bottom of the center unit. Press the seams to the outside.

14. Stitch one dark green and cream segment to each side of the center unit. Press the seams to the outside.

15. Stitch one navy 1½" x 12½" strip to the top and bottom of the center unit. Press the seams to the outside.

16. Stitch one navy and cream segment to each side of the center unit. Press the seams to the outside.

BLOCK 2 LAYOUT DIAGRAM

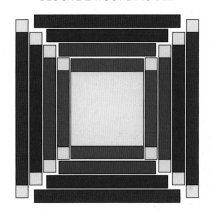

Quilt Top

1. Join the blocks to form three rows with a 1½" x 14½" gold sashing strip between each block and at the beginning and ending of each row. Refer to the Chickens on the Courthouse Steps Layout Diagram.

2. Press the seams toward the gold sashing strips.

3. Piece three gold strips and four 1½" cream squares as shown. Repeat to make four units. Press the seams toward the gold strips.

4. Join the gold sashing strips and rows to complete the quilt top.

5. Press the seams toward the gold strips.

3 ▭▭▭▭▭▭▭▭

Borders

1. Cut and piece together four navy border strips that measure 2½" x 46½".

2. Stitch one border strip to each side of the quilt top. Press the seams to the outside.

3. Stitch one cranberry cornerstone to each end of the remaining two navy border strips. Press the seams away from the cornerstones.

4. Stitch one navy and cranberry unit to the top and bottom of the quilt top. Press the seams to the outside.

FINISH

1. Layer the quilt top, batting and backing.
2. Quilt the piece as desired.

3. Bind the quilt with dark green fabric. See Chapter 1 for detailed instructions.

CHICKENS ON THE COURTHOUSE STEPS WALL HANGING LAYOUT DIAGRAM

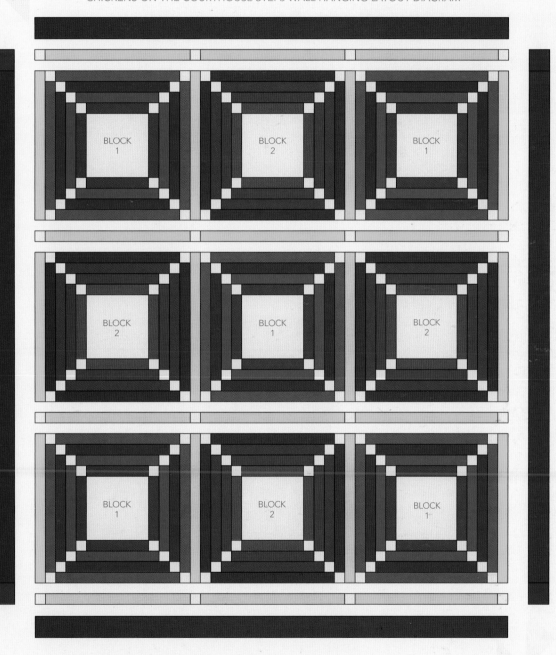

Cute as a Button Picture

This delightful project was inspired by a display at a fun little Amish resale shop. Some old buttons were sewn onto pieces of tagboard. I went home, pulled out my great-grandma's button jar and made my own Button Picture.

MATERIALS NEEDED

Dozens of buttons of varying sizes, colors and shapes

Frame

Mat board, cut to fill the frame

Cardboard, cut to fill the frame

Cutting board

Perle cotton thread

Large needle

Awl

Hammer

Thread

General sewing tools and supplies

STITCH

1. Place the mat board on top of the cutting board. If desired, put a piece of cardboard in between to protect the cutting board.

2. Lay the buttons on the mat board to get an idea for spacing. Punch holes every ¾" to 1½" all over the mat. Leave room around the edges for the frame.

3. Thread a large needle with heavy perle cotton, and tie a large knot in the end of the thread. Begin sewing the buttons on from the back of the mat board. Use a running stitch, and move from button to button. When you run out of thread, tie off, thread the needle with more heavy perle cotton thread and keep sewing until the mat board is covered to your taste.

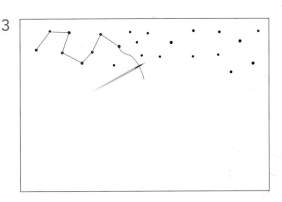

FINISH

1. Place the button-filled mat board inside the frame.

2. Place a layer of cardboard behind the mat board, and tack it in place. Hang your picture, or use an easel to display it.

If you want to follow a precise layout for your button art, you can use your digital camera to snap a picture of your final layout before you begin punching the holes for stitching. Or, cut a piece of paper that is the same size as the mat board surface within the framed area, and lay your buttons on that. Remove the buttons from the paper layout as you stitch them to the mat board.

Sharing Memories Album Cover

Everyone loves to look at family pictures. This quilted album cover offers a great way to show them off. Display your covered album on your coffee table and everyone will want a glimpse of your most precious possessions — your family and friends. **Finished cover size: 11" x 12½".**

MATERIALS NEEDED

1 gold fat quarter (blocks)

1 cranberry fat quarter (blocks)

1 blue fat quarter (blocks)

1 green fat quarter (blocks)

2 cream fat quarters (blocks)

½ yd. batting

¾ yd. print (backing, binding, tabs)

1½" or 2" three-ring binder, or a manufactured photo album of the same size

8 navy blue buttons

Thread

Gold-colored perle cotton thread

Large needle

General sewing tools and supplies

FABRIC	CUT	TO YIELD	FOR
Gold, cranberry, blue and green fat quarters	Layer the fat quarters; cut 3 strips, 2½" x 20"	12 strips	Blocks
2 cream fat quarters	Layer the fat quarters; cut 6 strips, 2½" x 20"	12 strips	Blocks
Print	Cut 4 strips, 1½" x 8"	4 strips	Tabs

STITCH

Strip Set 1

1. Stitch together Strip Set 1 in this order: cream, green, cream, blue, cream, green. Refer to the Strip Set 1 Layout Diagram.

2. Press the seams toward the green and blue strips.

3. Cut Strip Set 1 into five 2½"-wide segments. Refer to the Layout Diagram.

Strip Set 2

1. Stitch together Strip Set 2 in this order: gold, cream, cranberry, cream, gold, cream. Refer to the Strip Set 2 Layout Diagram.

2. Press the seams toward the gold and cranberry strips.

3. Cut Strip Set 2 into five 2½"-wide segments. Refer to the Layout Diagram.

Strip Set 3

1. Stitch together Strip Set 3 in this order: cream, blue, cream, green, cream, blue. Refer to the Strip Set 3 Layout Diagram.

2. Press the seams toward the blue and green strips.

3. Cut Strip Set 3 into five 2½"-wide segments. Refer to the Layout Diagram.

Strip Set 4

1. Stitch together a Strip Set 4 in this order: cranberry, cream, gold, cream, cranberry, cream. Refer to the Strip Set 4 Layout Diagram.

2. Press the seams toward the cranberry and gold strips.

3. Cut Strip Set 4 into five 2½"-wide segments. Refer to the Layout Diagram.

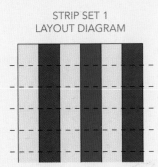

STRIP SET 1 LAYOUT DIAGRAM

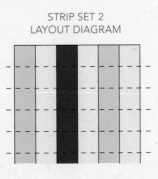

STRIP SET 2 LAYOUT DIAGRAM

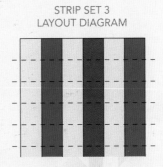

STRIP SET 3 LAYOUT DIAGRAM

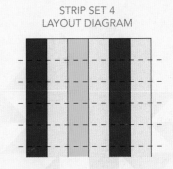

STRIP SET 4 LAYOUT DIAGRAM

Album Cover

1. Join the strip set segments together in order from Strip Set 1 to Strip Set 4. Repeat four more times until all of the strips are sewn together. Press the seams open. The finished length will be 40".

1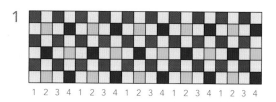

1 2 3 4 1 2 3 4 1 2 3 4 1 2 3 4 1 2 3 4

FINISH

Album Cover

1. Layer the quilt top, batting and backing.

2. Quilt the piece as desired. This project is a great one for you to practice quilting on your own machine.

3. Bind the quilted piece with a narrow navy binding. See Chapter 1 for detailed instructions.

Tab Closures

1. Fold one tab strip in half with right sides together so it measures 1½" x 4". Stitch the strip on the three open sides, ¼" from the edge; leave an opening on one side to turn the piece. Repeat to make four tabs.

2. Turn each tab right side out. Press. Slipstitch the opening closed.

1

OPEN

FOLD

Album

1. Wrap the finished cover around the open three-ring binder. Fold the outside edges in to gauge button and tab placement. Position the tabs in the middle of the outside corner squares, then fold to the other side as shown in the Sharing Memories Album Cover Construction Diagrams. Pin each tab in place.

2. Use the gold-colored perle cotton thread to stitch a button through the tab and one layer of the album cover. Repeat seven more times —two buttons per tab —for a total of eight buttons: four on the inside and four on the outside.

SHARING MEMORIES ALBUM COVER
CONSTRUCTION DIAGRAM, INSIDE

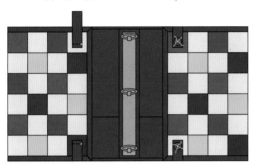

SHARING MEMORIES ALBUM COVER
CONSTRUCTION DIAGRAM, OUTSIDE

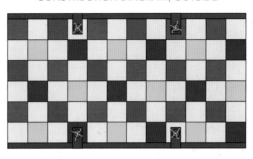

CHAPTER 5

Quilt a Bold Bedroom

The striking colors and rich florals used in these projects bring a bold look to a master or guest bedroom. If these colors don't fit your taste, experiment! Consider all-white or all-cream fabrics for a clean look; choose soft pastels to achieve an air of romance; or, pick a monochromatic palette for a tastefully sophisticated feel.

Pocket Full of Posies Quilt

When my quilter was working on this quilt, she just had to show it to everybody who stopped by. The most common comment was that it is a "happy" quilt, and I agree! I really enjoyed making this one. Because you mix and match the triangles, no two blocks are quite the same. It was really fun to see how each one turned out, and for a rather large quilt, it went together pretty fast. **Finished quilt size: 82" x 93". Finished block size: 8" x 8".**

MATERIALS NEEDED

5 red fat quarters (blocks)

5 blue fat quarters (blocks)

5 gold fat quarters (blocks)

5 green fat quarters (blocks)

3 yd. cream (blocks)

1 yd. small cream print (setting triangles, corner triangles)

3¼ yd. floral (blocks, second border)

½ yd. blue (first border)

1 yd. red (binding)

7½ yd. muslin (backing)

Queen- or king-size batting

Thread

General sewing tools and supplies

Note: The large floral print blocks are interspersed among the pieced blocks. If desired, create another set of pieced blocks in a fifth color; add five colored fat quarters and increase the yardage for the cream fabric to 4½ yd.

FABRIC	CUT	TO YIELD	FOR
Each of 5 red fat quarters	4 strips, 2⅜" x 18"; each cut to yield 6 squares, 2⅜" x 2⅜"; each cut once on the diagonal	240 triangles	Blocks
	2 strips, 1½" x 18"; each cut to yield 2 strips, 1½" x 6½" and 2 strips, 1½" x 18"	40 strips (discard 2 of each)	Blocks
Each of 5 blue fat quarters	4 strips, 2⅜" x 18"; each cut to yield 6 squares, 2⅜" x 2⅜"; each cut once on the diagonal	240 triangles	Blocks
	2 strips, 1½" x 18"; each cut to yield 2 strips, 1½" x 6½" and 2 strips, 1½" x 18"	40 strips (discard 2 of each)	Blocks
Each of 5 gold fat quarters	4 strips, 2⅜" x 18"; each cut to yield 6 squares, 2⅜" x 2⅜"; each cut once on the diagonal	240 triangles	Blocks
	2 strips, 1½" x 18"; each cut to yield 2 strips, 1½" x 6½" and 2 strips, 1½" x 18"	40 strips (discard 2 of each)	Blocks
Each of 5 green fat quarters	4 strips, 2⅜" x 18"; each cut to yield 6 squares, 2⅜" x 2⅜"; each cut once on the diagonal	240 triangles	Blocks
	2 strips, 1½" x 18"; each cut to yield 2 strips, 1½" x 6½" and 2 strips, 1½" x 18"	40 strips (discard 2 of each)	Blocks
Cream	8 selvage-to-selvage strips, 1½" wide; each cut again to yield 6 strips, 1½" x 6½"	48 strips	Blocks
	30 selvage-to-selvage strips, 2⅜" wide, each cut to yield 16 squares, 2⅜" x 2⅜", each cut once on the diagonal	960 triangles	Blocks
	12 selvage-to-selvage strips, 1½" wide, each cut again to yield 4 rectangles, 1½" x 8½"		Blocks
		48 rectangles	Blocks
Large floral	14 squares, 8½" x 8½"	14 squares	Blocks
Small cream print	6 squares, 12⅝" x 12⅝"; each cut twice on the diagonal	24 triangles (discard 2)	Side triangles
	2 squares, 6⅝" x 6⅝"; each cut once on the diagonal	4 triangles	Corner triangles

FAT QUARTER CUTTING DIAGRAM

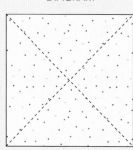

CREAM PRINT SIDE TRIANGLE CUTTING DIAGRAM

CREAM PRINT CORNER TRIANGLE CUTTING DIAGRAM

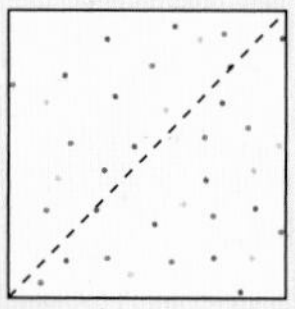

Blocks

1. Stitch one red 2⅜" triangle to one cream 2⅜" triangle along the diagonal edge to form a half-square triangle unit. Press the seams toward the red. Make 240 units.

2. Sew half of the triangle units together in pairs as shown. Press the seams to the left. Repeat to make 60 sets.

3. Sew the other half of the triangle units together in pairs as shown. Press the seams to the right. Repeat to make 60 sets.

4. Match one of the pairs from Step 2 with one of the pairs from Step 3 to make a four-patch unit as shown. Press the seams in a rotation; see Chapter 1 for detailed instructions. Repeat to make 60 four-patch units.

5. Mix and match the four-patch unit. Stitch together in sets rotating one of each set one quarter turn. Repeat to make 30 units.

6. Stitch together two of each of the four-patch units created in Step 5, rotating one four-patch unit by a one-half turn. Press the seams in a rotation. Stitch together 15 blocks as shown.

7. Stitch one cream 1½" x 6½" strip to each side of one of the blocks. Press the seams to the outside. Stitch one cream 1½" x 8½" strip to the top and bottom of the block. Repeat to make six blocks; these are the light-colored blocks.

8. Stitch one red 1½" x 6½" strip to each side of one block. Press the seams to the outside. Stitch one red 1½" x 8½" strip to the top and bottom of the block. Repeat to make nine blocks; these are the nine dark-colored blocks.

9. Repeat Steps 1 through 8 for the blue, gold, and green blocks. You will make 15 blocks of each color. You only need 14 blue blocks and 14 green blocks; use the two extra blocks for the Posy Pillows project.

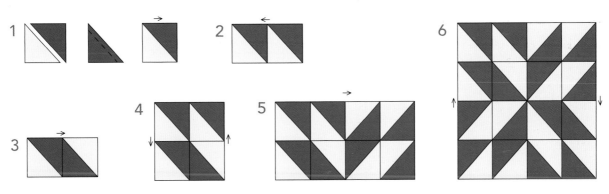

LIGHT-COLORED BLOCK
LAYOUT DIAGRAM

DARK-COLORED BLOCK
LAYOUT DIAGRAM

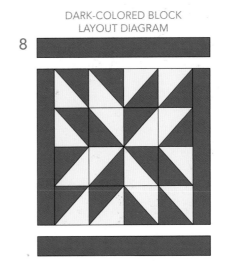

Quilt Top

1. Join the blocks together in diagonal rows as shown in the Pocket Full of Posies Quilt Layout Diagram. Stitch together the pieced blocks, setting triangles and 8½" large floral squares; begin and end each row with either a corner or side triangle. Press the seams toward the light-colored blocks and the outside triangles.

2. Join the rows together. Press the seams open so the seams will lay flat.

First Border

1. Measure the length of the quilt top. Cut and piece together two narrow blue borders that are 1½" wide and as long as the quilt top. Stitch one border to each side of the quilt top.

2. Measure the width of the quilt top. Cut and piece together two narrow blue borders that measure 1½" by the quilt top's width. Stitch one border each to the top and bottom edges of the quilt top.

Second Border

1. Measure the length of the quilt top that includes the first border. Cut and piece together two floral borders that measure 6½" and as long as the quilt top. Stitch one floral border to each side of the quilt top.

2. Measure the width of the quilt top that includes the first border. Cut and piece together two floral borders that measure 6½" and as long as the quilt top's width. Stitch one floral border to the top. Stitch one border each to the top and bottom edges of the quilt top.

FINISH

1. Layer the quilt top, batting and backing.
2. Quilt the piece as desired.

3. Bind the quilt with a narrow red binding. See Chapter 1 for detailed instructions.

Posy Pillows

These inviting pillows will add a punch of color to any bedroom. You can create them from scratch using the instructions that follow, or you can use up the two blocks left over from the Pocket Full of Posies Quilt. **Finished size: 18" x 18".**

MATERIALS NEEDED

(For two pillows)

2 pillow forms, 18" x 18"

2 green fat quarters* (center block, pillow top)

2 blue fat quarters* (center block, pillow top)

1 cream fat quarter (center blocks)

1 red fat quarter (pillow top)

1 yellow fat quarter (pillow top)

1¼ yd. batting

1¼ yd. muslin (lining)

1¼ yd. print (pillow backs)

½ yd. red (binding)

Thread

General sewing tools and supplies

*Note: Only 1 fat quarter is needed if you have blocks left over from the Pocket Full of Posies Quilt.

FABRIC	CUT	TO YIELD	FOR
1 blue and 1 green fat quarter, layered*	1 strip, 2⅜" x 20"; cut again to yield: • 8 squares, 2⅜" x 2⅜"; each cut in half on the diagonal	32 half-square triangles (16 blue and 16 green)	Blocks
	1 strip, 1½" x 20"; cut again to yield 2 strips, 1½" x 6½"	4 strips	Blocks
	1 strip, 1½" x 20"; cut again to yield 2 strips, 1½" x 8½"	4 strips	Blocks
1 cream fat quarter*	2 strips, 2⅜" x 20"; cut again to yield: • 8 squares, 2⅜" x 2⅜"; each cut in half on the diagonal	32 half-square triangles	Blocks
1 yellow fat quarter	4 squares, 6⅝" x 6⅝"; cut each on the diagonal	8 triangles	Side triangles
1 red fat quarter	2 strips, 2½" x 20"; cut each again into 8 squares, 2½" x 2½"	16 squares	Side triangles
1 blue and 1 green fat quarter, layered	2 strips, 1½" x 20"; cut again to yield 2 strips, 1½" x 16½"	4 strips	Borders
	2 strips, 1½" x 20"; cut again to yield 2 strips, 1½" x 18½"	4 strips	Borders
	2 squares, 8⅞" x 8⅞"; cut each in half on the diagonal	4 triangles	Side triangles

*Note: If you are using blocks left over from the Pocket Full of Posies Quilt, skip cutting steps marked with *.

STITCH

Blocks

Note: The instructions show how to make the blue block. Repeat the steps to make the green block. If you are using two blocks left over from the Pocket Full of Posies Quilt, skip to the next section.

1. Make half-square triangle units by stitching one blue 2⅜" half-square triangle to one cream 2⅜" half-square triangle ¼" from the diagonal edge. Press the seam toward the blue. Repeat to make 16 units.

2. Sew eight triangle units together in pairs as shown. Press the seams to the left. Repeat to make four sets.

3. Sew the other eight triangle units together in pairs as shown. Press the seams to the right. Repeat to make four sets.

4. Stitch together one unit from Step 2 to a unit from Step 3 as shown. Press the seams in a rotation; see Chapter 1 for detailed instructions. Repeat to make four four-patch units.

5. Stitch together two of the four-patch units in sets, rotating one unit by one quarter turn. Repeat to make two units.

1   2   3

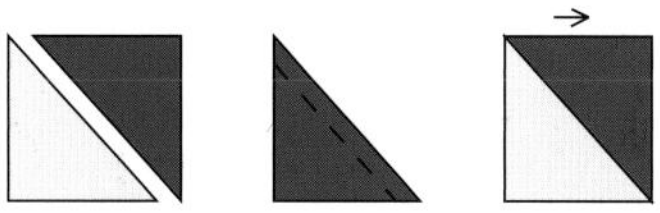

4 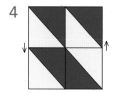 5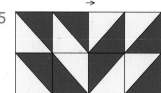

6. Stitch together the two units from Step 5, rotating one unit by one half turn. Press the seams in a rotation; see Chapter 1 for detailed instructions. Make one block.

7. Stitch one blue 1½" x 6½" strip to each side of the block. Press the seams to the outside. Stitch one blue 1½" x 8½" strip to the top and another to the bottom of the block. Press the seams to the outside.

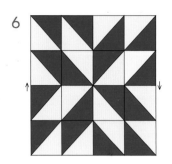

Side Triangles and Borders

1. Use a pencil to draw a diagonal line on the wrong side of each of the red 2½" squares. Lay one red square right sides together on the outside corner of one yellow triangle. Stitch on the diagonal line.

2. Trim the outside points to within ¼" of the stitching line.

3. Fold the piece open, and press the seams to the outside.

4. Repeat Steps 1 through 3 to make eight yellow, four green and four blue units.

5. Stitch one yellow triangle unit to each side of the blue block. Press the seams to the outside. Repeat for the green block.

6. Stitch one yellow triangle to the top and the bottom of the blue block. Press the seams to the outside. Repeat for the green block.

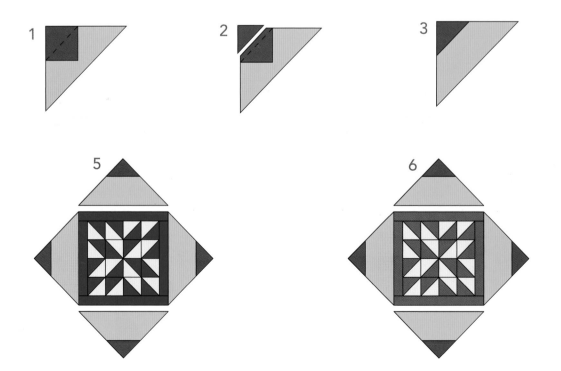

7. Stitch one large blue triangle to each side of the green block. Press the seams to the outside. Repeat for the top and bottom of the block.

8. Stitch one large green triangle to each side of the blue block. Press the seams to the outside. Repeat for the top and bottom of the block.

9. Stitch one blue 1½" x 16½" border strip to each side of the blue block. Press the seams to the outside.

10. Stitch one blue 1½" x 18½" strip to the top and bottom of the blue block. Press the seams to the outside.

11. Stitch one green 1½" x 16½" strip to each side of the green block. Press the seams to the outside.

12. Stitch one green 1½" x 18½" strip to the top and bottom of the green block. Press the seams to the outside.

7

8

FINISH

Quilting

1. Layer the pillow top, batting and lining.

2. Quilt the piece as desired.

Pillow

1. Cut four pieces that measure 12" x the quilted pillow top measurement.

2. For each backing piece, press one long side under by ¼". Repeat. Stitch ⅛" away from the folded edge.

3. Overlap two backing pieces with the finished edges in the middle. Lay the pieces wrong sides together on the back of the quilted pillow top. Make sure that the edges match all the way around.

4. Baste all of the layers together close to the edge as shown.

5. Bind the pillow with a narrow red binding. See Chapter 1 for detailed instructions.

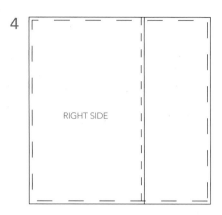

POSY PILLOW LAYOUT DIAGRAM, BLUE BLOCK TOP

POSY PILLOW LAYOUT DIAGRAM, GREEN BLOCK TOP

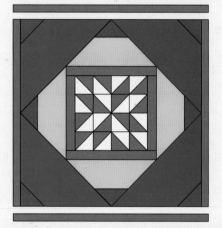

Darling Dresser Scarf

This versatile project adds pizazz to your dresser, but it doesn't take long to complete. Add or delete blocks to customize the length. If you have a favorite 10" x 10" block, you can substitute that one, instead. **Finished size: 14" x 56". Finished block size: 10" x 10".**

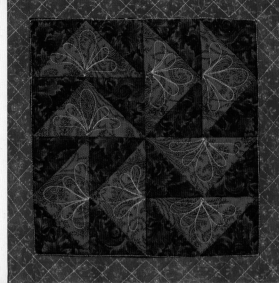

MATERIALS NEEDED

1 red fat quarter (blocks)

1 yellow fat quarter (blocks)

1 green fat quarter (blocks)

1 blue fat quarter (blocks)

¾ yd. floral print (setting triangles)

½ yd. red (binding)

1 yd. batting

1 yd. muslin (backing)

Thread

General sewing tools and supplies

FABRIC	CUT	TO YIELD	FOR
Red fat quarter	2 strips, 2⅞" x 18"; cut each strip again to yield 8 squares, 2⅞" x 2⅞"; cut each square in half on the diagonal	16 triangles	Blocks
	1 strip, 5¼" x 18"; cut the strip again to yield 2 squares, 5¼" x 5¼"; cut each square in half twice on the diagonal	8 triangles	Blocks
	2 strips, 1½" x 8½"	2 strips	Blocks
	2 strips, 1½" x 10½"	2 strips	Blocks
Yellow fat quarter	2 strips, 2⅞" x 18"; cut each strip again to yield 8 squares, 2⅞" x 2⅞"; cut each square in half on the diagonal	16 triangles	Blocks
	1 strip, 5¼" x 18"; cut the strip again to yield 2 squares, 5¼" x 5¼"; cut each square in half twice on the diagonal	8 triangles	Blocks
	2 strips, 1½" x 8½"	2 strips	Blocks
	2 strips, 1½" x 10½"	2 strips	Blocks
Green fat quarter	2 strips, 2⅞" x 18"; cut each strip again to yield 8 squares, 2⅞" x 2⅞"; cut each square in half on the diagonal	16 triangles	Blocks
	1 strip, 5¼" x 18"; cut the strip again to yield 2 squares, 5¼" x 5¼"; cut each square in half twice on the diagonal	8 triangles	Blocks
	2 strips, 1½" x 8½"	2 strips	Blocks
	2 strips, 1½" x 10½"	2 strips	Blocks
Blue fat quarter	2 strips, 2⅞" x 18"; cut each strip again to yield 8 squares, 2⅞" x 2⅞"; cut each square in half on the diagonal	16 triangles	Blocks
	1 strip, 5¼" x 18"; cut the strip again to yield 2 squares, 5¼" x 5¼"; cut each square in half twice on the diagonal	8 triangles	Blocks
	2 strips, 1½" x 8½"	2 strips	Blocks
	2 strips, 1½" x 10½"	2 strips	Blocks
Floral print	2 squares, 15½" x 15½"; cut each square in half twice on the diagonal	8 triangles; discard 2	Side triangles
	2 squares, 8" x 8"; cut each square in half once on the diagonal	4 triangles	Corner triangles

Layer and cut through all of the fat quarters at once to save cutting time. Then mix and match the backgrounds, triangles and borders to make each block different.

STITCH

Blocks

Note: The instructions show the red and yellow block. Repeat Steps 1 through 8 to complete all four blocks total.

1. Match up the center triangles and background triangles as shown.

2. With right sides together, lay a background triangle on the diagonal edge of a center triangle. Stitch ¼" from edges as shown. Trim the point, and press the piece to the outside.

3. Repeat Steps 1 and 2 for the other side of the unit. Repeat to make eight units for each block of the dresser runner.

4. Stitch the triangle units together in pairs as shown. Repeat to make four pairs.

5. Rotate one pair by a quarter turn. Stitch two pairs together. Make two sets for each block.

6. Rotate a set by a half turn. Stitch the two sets together to create the final block; refer to the Block Layout Diagram.

7. Stitch one 1½" x 8½" strip to the top and bottom of the block; refer to the Block Layout Diagram. Press the seams away from the block.

8. Stitch a 1½" x 10½" strip to either side of the block. Press the seams away from the block.

1   2   3

4 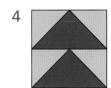   5  6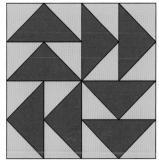

Quilt Top

1. Join the blocks, side and corner triangles in diagonal rows as shown in the Darling Dresser Scarf Layout Diagram. Press the seams toward the triangles.

2. Join the rows together. Press the seams open so the seams will lay flat.

FINISH

1. Layer the dresser scarf top, batting and backing.

2. Quilt the piece as desired.

3. Bind the scarf with a narrow red binding. See Chapter 1 for detailed instructions.

BLOCK LAYOUT DIAGRAM

DARLING DRESSER SCARF LAYOUT DIAGRAM

Framed Flowers

Every year for Christmas, I try to make something special for my husband's mother and grandmother. This past year, I made these same small quilts to match the colors in their homes. The frames really helped to show off the quilts. **Finished size: 8" x 20". Finished block size: 3" x 3".**

MATERIALS NEEDED

8" x 20" frame

1 green fat quarter (inner border)

1 cream print fat quarter (blocks, side triangles, corner triangles)

1 gold print fat quarter (borders)

Scraps of red, blue and gold (blocks)

¼ yd. blue (binding)

⅓ yd. muslin (backing)

⅓ yd. batting

Thread

General sewing tools and supplies

FABRIC	CUT	TO YIELD	FOR
Cream fat quarter	2 squares, 2¾" x 2¾"; cut each square twice on the diagonal	8 triangles	Block
	4 squares, 2" x 2"	4 squares	Block
	2 squares, 5½" x 5½"; cut each square twice on the diagonal	8 triangles; discard 2	Side triangles
	2 squares, 3" x 3"	4 triangles	Corner triangles
Green fat quarter	1 strip, 2" x 17"	1 strip	Inner border
	2 squares, 2⅜" x 2⅜"; cut each square in half on the diagonal	4 triangles	Block
Red scrap	2 squares, 2⅜" x 2⅜"; cut each square in half on the diagonal	4 triangles	Block
	1 square, 2¾" x 2¾"; cut it in half on the diagonal twice	4 triangles	Block
Blue scrap	2 squares, 2⅜" x 2⅜"; cut each square in half on the diagonal	4 triangles	Block
	1 square, 2¾" x 2¾"; cut it in half on the diagonal twice	4 triangles	Block
Gold scrap	2 squares, 2⅜" x 2⅜"; cut each square in half on the diagonal	4 triangles	Block
Gold print fat quarter	2 strips, 2½" x 17"	2 strips	Borders
	2 strips, 2½" x 10¾"	2 strips	Borders

STITCH

Blocks

Note: Instructions are given for one block. Repeat to create a total of four identical blocks.

1. Stitch one small red triangle to the left side of one cream triangle as shown. Press open.

2. Stitch one unit from Step 1 to a large red triangle as shown. Press open.

3. Repeat Steps 1 and 2, this time using blue and cream triangles.

4. Stitch one cream 2" square to the right side of the red square unit created in Step 2. Press the seams to the left.

5. Stitch one green triangle to one gold triangle. Press the seams open.

6. Stitch the yellow and green triangle unit to the left side of the blue unit created in Step 3. Press the seams to the right.

7. Stitch the unit created in Step 4 to the unit created in Step 6 as shown. Press the seams in a rotation; see Chapter 1 for detailed instructions.

1

2

3

4

5

6

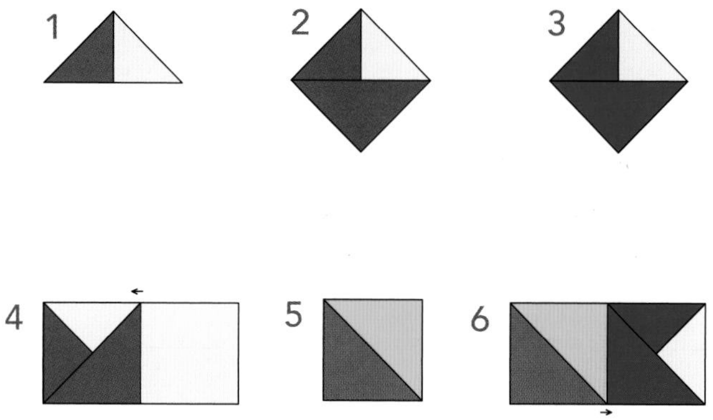

BLOCK LAYOUT DIAGRAM

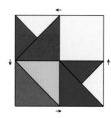

Side and Corner Triangles

1. Join the blocks, side triangles and corner triangles in diagonal rows, as shown in the Framed Flowers Diagram. Press the seams toward the cream triangles.

2. Join the rows together. Press the seams open so the seams will lay flat.

Borders

1. Stitch the 2" x 17" green strip to the bottom of the quilt center as shown in the Framed Flowers Layout Diagram. Press the seams toward the green strip.

2. Stitch one 2½" x 17" gold strip to the top and the bottom of the quilt center. Press toward the gold strip.

3. Stitch one 2½" x 10¾" gold strip to either side as shown. Press the seams toward the gold strip. The quilt will be oversized to allow for quilting and then trimming to fit the frame.

FINISH

1. Layer the quilt top, batting and backing.

2. Quilt the piece as desired.

3. Trim the oversized piece to fit the frame.

4. If desired, bind the piece. Binding is optional; see Chapter 1 for detailed instructions on binding.

5. Frame the quilt.

FRAMED FLOWERS CONSTRUCTION LAYOUT DIAGRAM

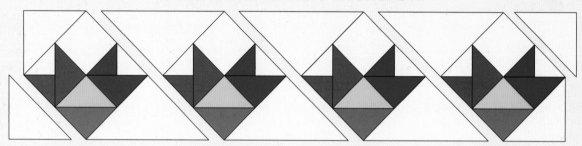

FRAMED FLOWERS LAYOUT DIAGRAM

CHAPTER 6

Style a Lovely Living Room

Pricey knickknacks, formal furniture and carpets in "don't-get-dirty" colors often turn living rooms into museums that families only enter when company comes calling. But you don't have to trade a warm, welcoming look for sophistication and elegance. These projects in black, red, green, taupe and cream balance classic good looks with comfort and charm. Or, mix and match colors and fabrics to achieve the perfect look for your décor.

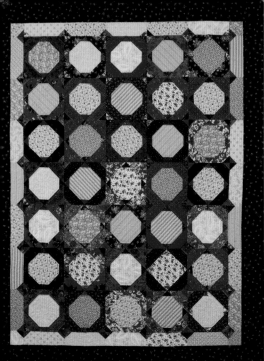

Graceful Centers Lap Quilt

I designed this quilt with a friend's living room in mind. She has taupe walls and cream leather sofas. The deep, rich colors of the quilt and coordinating pieces really made the room a knockout! **Finished quilt size: 61" x 79". Finished block size: 9" x 9".**

MATERIALS NEEDED

4 red fat quarters (blocks)

4 green fat quarters (blocks)

4 black fat quarters (blocks)

12 cream fat quarters (blocks)

1½ yd. black print (borders)

1 yd. red (binding)

5¼ yd. print or solid (backing)

Twin-size batting

Thread

General sewing tools and supplies

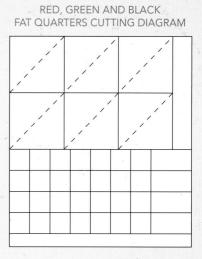

FABRIC	CUT	TO YIELD	FOR
Each of 4 red, green and black fat quarters	2 strips, 5⅜" x 18"; cut each strip again into 3 squares, 5⅜" x 5⅜", and cut each square on the diagonal	144 triangles	Blocks
	4 strips, 2" x 18"; cut each strip again into 7 squares, 2" x 2"	336 squares	Blocks and border
Each of 9 cream fat quarters	2 strips, 6⅞" x 18"; cut each strip again into 2 squares, 6⅞" x 6⅞"	36 squares; discard 1	Center squares
	1 strip, 3½" x 20"; cut each strip into 2 rectangles, 3½" x 9½"	18 rectangles	Border
Each of 3 cream fat quarters	1 strip, 3½" x 20"; cut each strip into 2 rectangles, 3½" x 9½"	6 rectangles	Border
	1 square, 3½" x 3½"	4 squares	Border corners

STITCH

Blocks

1. Draw a diagonal line on the wrong side of each 2" square.

2. Divide the large triangles into matching groups of four. Divide the 2" squares into matching groups of four.

3. Mix and match pieces into groups for 35 different blocks. Each block should have: one cream center block, four large matching triangles, and two sets of four matching 2" squares. Refer to the Block Component Diagram.

4. Set aside the remaining 2" squares (there should be 52) for the inside border.

5. Lay one 2" square right sides together on each corner of one 6⅞" cream center square. Stitch on the diagonal lines.

6. Trim extra layers of fabric to ¼".

7. Press the seams to the outside. Repeat Steps 5 through 7 to make 35 blocks.

8. Lay one 2" square right sides together on the outside corner of one of the large triangles. Stitch on the diagonal lines.

9. Trim extra layers of fabric to ¼".

10. Press the seams to the outside. Make four for each block.

11. Stitch one large triangle unit to each side of the block center; refer to the Block Construction Diagram. Press the seams to the outside. Stitch one large triangle unit to the top and bottom of the block center. Press the seams to the outside. Repeat to make 35 blocks.

BLOCK COMPONENT DIAGRAM

BLOCK CONSTRUCTION DIAGRAM

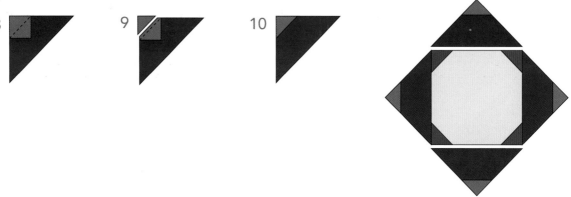

Quilt Top

1. Measure the blocks. If any blocks measure more than 9½" square, trim them to 9½" square. If any blocks are less than 9½" square, trim the length of each border strip to match the blocks.

2. Join the blocks in rows, alternating block colors. Refer to the Graceful Centers Lap Quilt Layout Diagram, but don't worry about matching the illustration exactly. Avoid placing identical blocks next to each other. Press the seams open.

3. Stitch the rows together. Press the seams open so they will lay flat.

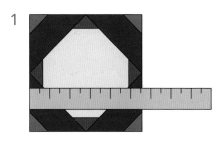

First Border

1. Lay one 2" square on opposite corners of one 9½" border strip; the 2" squares do not need to match. Stitch on the diagonal lines.

2. Trim the extra layers of fabric to ¼".

3. Press the seams to the outside. Repeat to make 24 border strips.

4. Lay one 2" square right sides together on one corner of each 3½" corner square. Stitch on the diagonal lines. Trim extra layers of fabric to ½". Press the seams to the outside. Repeat to make four units for the corners of the borders.

5. Stitch seven border strips together. Repeat to make a second seven-strip unit. Press the seams open.

6. Stitch one of the seven-strip border units to each side of the quilt top. Position the triangles to the inside; refer to the Graceful Centers Lap Quilt Layout Diagram. The triangles will match up with the triangles in the quilt center to form diamonds.

7. Stitch five border strips together. Stitch one 3½" corner strip with a triangle to each end of the five-strip unit. Repeat to make a second unit. Press the seams open.

8. Stitch one five-strip unit to the top and one to the bottom of the quilt top. The triangles will match up to create diamonds.

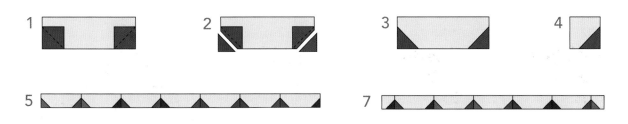

Second Border

1. Measure the length and width of the quilt top to make sure the cutting measurements will work for your quilt.

2. Cut and piece together two black borders that measure 5½" x 69½"; if necessary, adjust the border measurements to fit your quilt. Stitch one border to each side of the quilt top. Press the seams toward the outside.

3. Cut and piece together two black borders that measure 5½" x 61½"; if necessary, adjust the border measurements to fit your quilt. Stitch one border to the top and another to the bottom of the quilt top. Press the seams toward the outside.

FINISH

1. Layer the quilt top, batting and backing.

2. Quilt the piece as desired.

3. Bind the quilt with a narrow red binding. See Chapter 1 for detailed instructions.

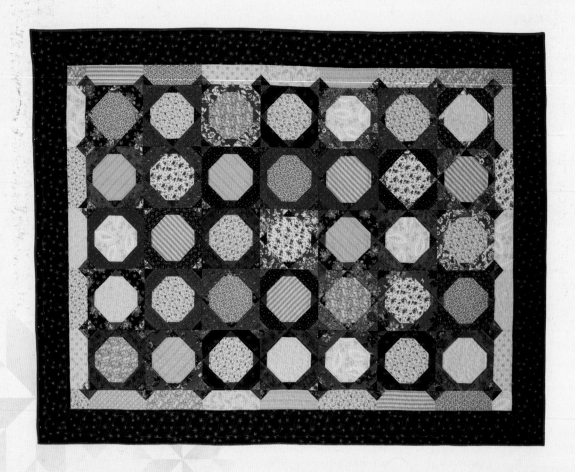

GRACEFUL CENTERS LAP QUILT LAYOUT DIAGRAM

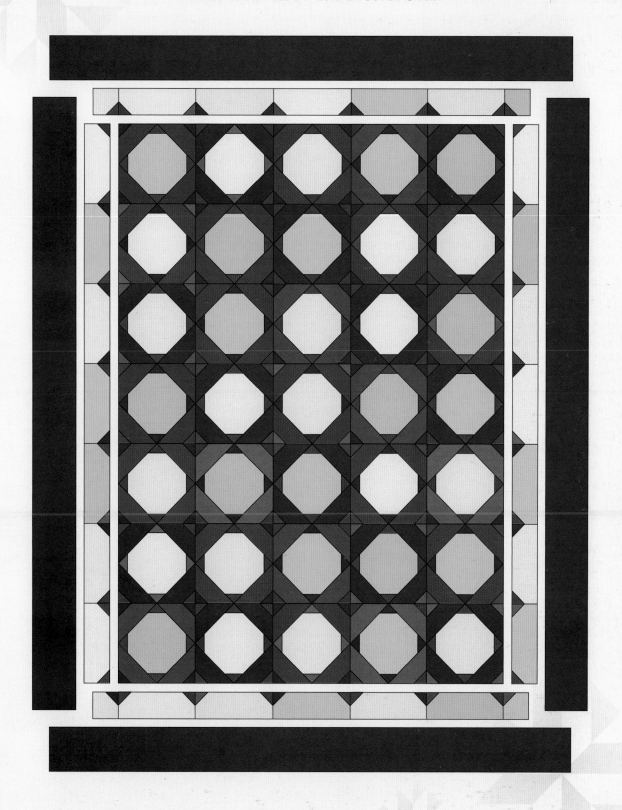

Coffee and Cocktails Table Runner

This project can be used in so many ways. It's a perfect runner for your coffee, sofa or cocktail table, but you also can drape it over your fireplace mantel or use it to adorn the back of your sofa. **Finished runner size: 14" x 42". Finished block size: 10" x 10".**

MATERIALS NEEDED

1 red fat quarter (blocks)

1 green fat quarter (blocks)

1 black fat quarter (blocks)

1 tan fat quarter (setting triangles)

½ yd. black (binding)

1 yd. print (backing)

1 yd. batting

Thread

General sewing tools and supplies

FABRIC	CUT	TO YIELD	FOR
Red fat quarter	1 square, 6½" x 6½"	1 square	Center square
	2 rectangles, 2½" x 10½"	2 rectangles	Border
	2 rectangles, 2½" x 6½"	2 rectangles	Border
	4 squares, 2½" x 2½"	4 squares	Blocks
	2 squares, 3½" x 3½"	2 squares	Connecting blocks
Green fat quarter	1 square, 6½" x 6½"	1 square	Center square
	2 rectangles, 2½" x 10½"	2 rectangles	Border
	2 rectangles, 2½" x 6½"	2 rectangles	Border
	4 squares, 2½" x 2½"	4 squares	Blocks
	2 squares, 3½" x 3½"	2 squares	Connecting blocks
Black fat quarter	1 square, 6½" x 6½"	1 square	Center square
	2 rectangles, 2½" x 10½"	2 rectangles	Border
	2 rectangles, 2½" x 6½"	2 rectangles	Border
	4 squares, 2½" x 2½"	4 squares	Blocks
Tan fat quarter	1 square, 15½" x 15½"; cut again twice on the diagonal	4 triangles	Setting triangles

STITCH

Blocks

1. Draw one diagonal line on the wrong side of each 2½" square.

2. Divide the cut pieces into three piles, with the following in each pile: one center square, four small corner triangles, two border rectangles that measure 2½" x 10½" and two border rectangles that measure 2½" x 6½".

3. Lay one 2½" square right sides together on each corner of one 6½" center square. Stitch on the diagonal lines.

4. Trim the extra layers of fabric to ¼".

5. Press the seams to the outside.

6. Stitch one 2½" x 6½" rectangle to each side of the block center. Stitch one 2½" x 10½" rectangle to the top and another to the bottom. Press the seams to the outside.

7. Repeat Steps 3 through 6 for the two remaining blocks.

1

3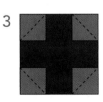

4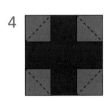

5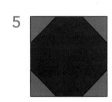

6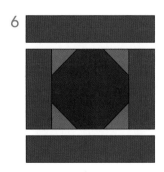

Setting Triangles

1. Draw a diagonal line on the wrong side of each 3½" square.

2. Lay one 3½" square right sides together on the outside corner of one setting triangle. Stitch on the diagonal line.

3. Trim the extra layers of fabric to ¼".

4. Press the seams to the outside. Repeat for all four setting triangles.

5. Join the blocks and side triangles in diagonal rows as shown in the Coffee and Cocktails Table Runner Layout Diagram. Match the red and tan setting triangles and the two green and tan setting triangles as shown. Press the seams open.

1   2 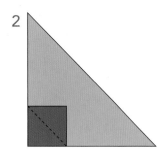   3 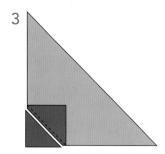   4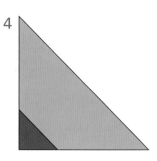

FINISH

1. Layer the top, batting and backing.

2. Quilt the piece as desired.

3. Bind the runner with a narrow black binding. See Chapter 1 for detailed instructions.

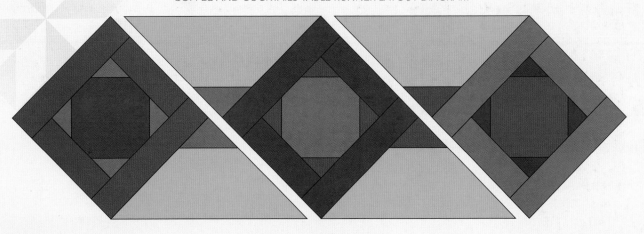

Waves of Mercy Wall Hanging

This little piece makes a lovely statement. It's really just a simple center block with borders that set it off, but it's also a great way to practice stitching flying geese units. **Finished wall hanging size: 22" x 22".**

MATERIALS NEEDED

1 red fat quarter (block and borders)

1 green fat quarter (block and borders)

1 black fat quarter (block and borders; this must be at least 21" long)

2 cream fat quarters (block)

Scrap of black (center block)

⅜ yd. red (binding)

¾ yd. print (backing)

¾ batting

Thread

General sewing tools and supplies

FABRIC	CUT	TO YIELD	FOR
Red fat quarter	1 strip, 2½" x 20"; cut again into 8 squares 2½" x 2½"	8 squares	Block
	1 strip, 2⅞" x 20"; cut again into 6 squares, 2⅞" x 2⅞"; cut each square once on the diagonal	12 triangles	Block
	1 strip, 1½" x 20"; cut again into 12 squares, 1½" x 1½"	12 squares	Block
	4 strips, 1½" x 16½"	4 strips	Borders
Green fat quarter	1 strip, 2½" x 20"; cut again into 8 squares 2½" x 2½"	8 squares	Block
	1 strip, 2⅞" x 20"; cut again into 6 squares, 2⅞" x 2⅞"; cut each square on the diagonal	12 triangles	Block
	1 strip, 1½" x 20"; cut again into 12 squares, 1½" x 1½"	12 squares	Block
	4 strips, 1½" x 18½"	4 strips	Borders
Black fat quarter	1 strip, 2½" x 21"; cut again into 8 squares 2½" x 2½"	8 squares	Block
	1 strip, 2⅞" x 21"; cut again into 6 squares, 2⅞" x 2⅞"; cut each square on the diagonal	12 triangles	Block
	1 strip, 1½" x 21"; cut again into 12 squares, 1½" x 1½"	12 squares	Block
	4 strips, 1½" x 20½"	4 strips	Borders
Cream fat quarters	12 rectangles, 2½" x 4½"	12 rectangles	Flying geese
	3 strips, 2⅞" x 20"; cut each strip into 6 squares, 2⅞" x 2⅞"; cut each square on the diagonal	36 triangles	Block
	1 strip, 1½" x 20"; cut again into 12 squares, 1½" x 1½"	12 squares	Border
Scrap of black fabric	1 square, 4½" x 4½"	1 square	Center block

STITCH

Flying Geese

Note: The instructions show how to make one red flying geese unit. Repeat Steps 2 through 7 to create four red, four green and four black flying geese units.

1. Draw a diagonal line on the wrong side of eight red, eight green and eight black 2½" squares.

2. Lay one 2½" red square right sides together on one end of one 2½" x 4½" cream rectangle. Stitch on the diagonal line.

3. Trim the extra layers of fabric to ¼".

4. Press the seam to the outside.

5. Lay one red 2½" square right sides together on the other end of the cream rectangle. Stitch on the diagonal line.

6. Trim the extra layers of fabric to ¼".

7. Press the seam to the outside.

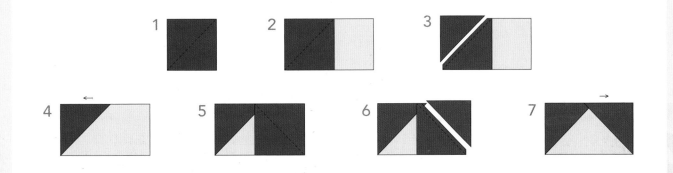

Half-Square Triangle Units

1. Stitch one green 2⅞" triangle to one cream 2⅞" triangle, ¼" away from the diagonal edge. Press the seam toward the green.

2. Repeat Step 1 to create a total of 36 half-square triangle units: 12 green and cream, 12 red and cream and 12 black and cream.

Quilt Top

1. Stitch flying geese units together in sets of three in this order: red, green and black. Repeat to make four sets.

2. Stitch half-square triangle units together in rows of three as follows, making sure the triangles all point in the same direction: Row 1: black, green, red; Row 2: green, red, black; and Row 3: red, black, green. Press all of the seams open.

3. Repeat Step 2 to make four sets of each row.

4. Stitch the rows together as shown. Press seams open. Repeat to make four half-square triangle blocks.

5. Stitch the half-square triangle blocks, flying geese units and center block together in rows as shown in the Block Diagram. Note that the half-square triangle units always have the cream triangles nearest to the middle of the wall hanging. Press the seams open.

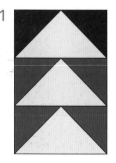

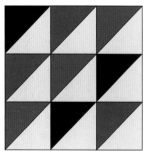

BLOCK DIAGRAM

Borders

1. Draw a diagonal line on the wrong side of eight 1½" cream squares. Set the remaining squares aside.

2. Lay one 1½" cream square right sides together on each end of one 1½" x 16½" red border strip. Stitch on the diagonal lines.

3. Trim extra layers of fabric to ¼".

4. Press seams to the outside. Repeat to make four red and cream border strips.

5. Set two red and cream border strips aside. To the other two strips, stitch a 1½" cream square to each end of two of the red border strips as shown. Press the seams away from the small cream squares.

6. Repeat Steps 1 through 5 for green strips; use red squares instead of cream squares.

7. Repeat Steps 1 through 5 for the black strips, use green squares instead of cream squares.

8. Stitch one short red border to each side of the quilt top. Press the seams to the outside.

9. Stitch one red border with corner squares to the top of the quilt top and another to the bottom of the quilt top. Press the seams to the outside.

10. Repeat Steps 8 and 9 to add the green borders, then the black borders. Refer to the Waves of Mercy Wall Hanging Layout Diagram.

FINISH

1. Layer the quilt top, batting and backing.

2. Quilt the piece as desired.

3. Bind the quilt with red binding. See Chapter 1 for detailed instructions.

WAVES OF MERCY WALL HANGING LAYOUT DIAGRAM

Treasure Boxes

Have enough time to wrap a present? That's all the time you need to make one of these beautiful storage boxes for your photos, memories or anything else you want to keep handy and organized. These easy-to-make boxes look great, and they are so useful, too. **Finished box size: 11" x 7½" x 4½".**

MATERIALS NEEDED

(For one Treasure Box)

Photo storage box, 11" x 7½" x 4½"

Paper-backed fusible web

Fabric glue

2 coordinating fat quarters (box, lid)

Screwdriver or other tool to remove box tag

General sewing tools and supplies

FABRIC	CUT	TO YIELD	FOR
Fat quarter 1	1 rectangle, 12" x 16"	1 rectangle	Box top
Fat quarter 2	1 rectangle, 18" x 20"; cut again in half lengthwise	2 rectangles	Box sides and bottom

STITCH

1. Stitch the 9" ends of the two 9" x 20" rectangles together to create a 9" x 40" rectangle.

2. Press the seam open.

1

COVER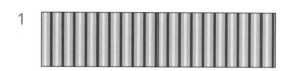
Box

1. Remove the label holder from the front of the box. If it comes off easily, you can reattach it later, if desired.

2. Apply fusible web to the wrong side of both pieces of fabric; follow the manufacturer's instructions.

3. Wrap the 9" x 40" fabric piece all the way around the sides of the box. Overlap the edges at the final corner, and fold the fabric edge under ¼". Trim if necessary. Fuse the fabric in place.

4. Fold the lower edges of the fabric over the bottom of the box like you would to wrap a present. Fuse the fabric in place.

5. Fold the upper edges of the fabric to the inside of the box. Fuse in place.

6. Use fabric glue to secure any edges that are not fused down.

7. If desired, reattach the label holder.

3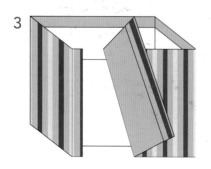

4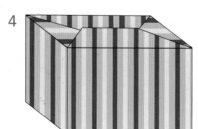

5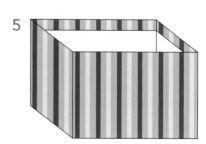

Lid

1. Lay the box lid on the wrong side of the 12" x 16" rectangle; position the lid so there is an equal amount of fabric on each side and on the top and bottom.

2. Fold the fabric edges to the inside of the box; trim the extra fabric at the corners if necessary.

3. Fuse the fabric in place.

4. Use fabric glue to secure any edges that are not fused down.

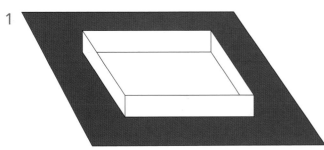

Colorful Canvases

So many fabrics are simply stunning and elegant on their own. This quick, easy project lets you put some fabrics that are just too pretty to cut in the spotlight as artwork. **Finished canvas size: 14" x 14".**

MATERIALS NEEDED

(For one canvas)

14" x 14" stretched canvas (foundation)

1 fat quarter (canvas cover)

2 yd. coordinating trim (trim)

Staple gun and staples

Fabric glue

General sewing tools and supplies

FABRIC	CUT	TO YIELD	FOR
Fat quarter	1 square, 18" x 18"	1 square	Canvas cover

COVER

1. Place the canvas right side down on top of the wrong side of the 18" square.

2. Fold two opposite sides of fabric over the edges of the frame of the canvas. Use the staple gun to staple the edges in place; keep the fabric taut.

3. Fold in the corners of the other two sides as shown.

4. Fold the other sides over the edges of the frame. Use the staple gun to staple the edges in place; keep the fabric taut.

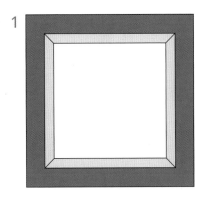

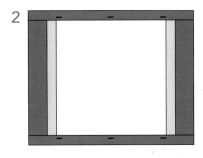

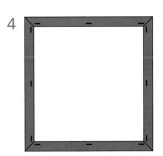

EMBELLISH

1. Use a pencil and ruler to draw a line on the right side of the fabric 2" from the edge. Repeat for each side of the canvas to make four lines as shown.

2. On the back of the canvas, make marks 2" from each edge as shown.

3. Cut the trim into 18" lengths.

4. Lay one piece of trim along one of the pencil lines. Wrap it around to the back of the canvas, and staple the ends of the trim in place. Repeat using the other line that is parallel to the first one.

5. Lay two more pieces of trim along the other two pencil lines. Position the new piece of trim so one end overlaps the trim that is already in place and the other runs beneath the trim that is already in place. Wrap the edges around to the back. Staple the trim in place as shown. Repeat for the remaining piece of trim.

6. Run a line of fabric glue under the trim on the front to keep it from slipping out of place.

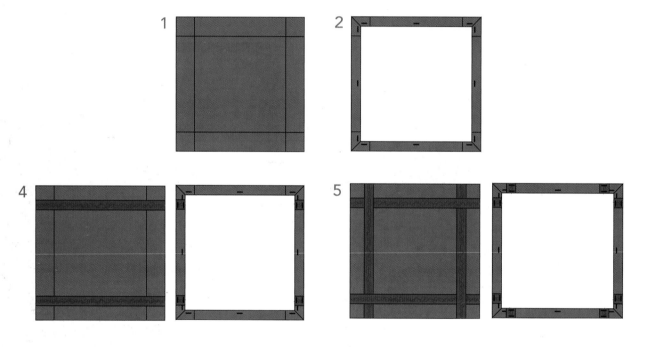

CHAPTER 7

Create a Colorful Kid's Room

I love making kid's quilts more than any other type. When I choose my fabric, I try to soften the color palette, but it just doesn't happen. Bright colors are just too much fun to work with! I love to mix and match all of the dazzling, whimsical prints and come up with something that really says, "Wow!"

Delightful Patches Bed Quilt

This fun kid's quilt is so easy to make, and it stitches up in a flash. It looks just like a scrap quilt, but it's made with fun, funky fat quarters. These bright pastels will really liven up your little one's room. **Finished quilt size: 68" x 86".** **Finished block size: 6" x 6".**

MATERIALS NEEDED

18 bright pastel fat quarters (blocks)

1 lime green fat quarter (cornerstones)

½ yd. yellow (first border)

¾ yd. teal (second border)

1¼ yd. multicolored print (outside border)

1 yd. pink (binding)

5½ yd. print (backing)

Twin-size batting

General sewing tools and supplies

FABRIC	CUT	TO YIELD	FOR
Each of 18 bright pastel fat quarters	2 strips, 6½" x 18"; cut each strip again into 2 squares, 6½" x 6½"	72 squares	Blocks
	3 strips*, 2½" x 18"; cut each strip again into 6 squares, 2½" x 2½"	324 squares	Blocks
Lime green fat quarter	4 squares, 7½" x 7½"	4 squares	Cornerstones

*If you can't cut a third 2½" strip from the fat quarters because they aren't long enough, cut the last 2½" squares from scraps left over after cutting the larger squares.

FAT QUARTER CUTTING DIAGRAM

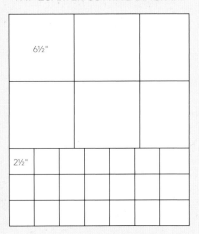

6½"

2½"

STITCH

Blocks

1. Stitch 2½" squares together in groups of three; just mix and match the small squares without worrying too much about which squares go where. Repeat to make 108 three-square units. Press the seams to one side.

2. Stitch three of the three-strip sets together to create a nine-patch block. Repeat to make 36 nine-patch blocks.

3. Press the seams open or to one side, whichever you prefer. Alternate the way the squares are pressed so the seams will lay flat.

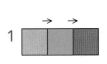

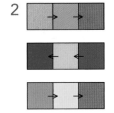

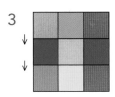

Quilt Top

1. Stitch three nine-patch blocks and six 6½" squares together in horizontal rows; refer to the Delightful Patches Bed Quilt Layout Diagram.

2. Press the seams in rows in opposite directions so the seams will lay flat when the rows are stitched together.

3. Stitch the rows together; refer to the Layout Diagram. Press the seams open or to one side.

Borders

1. Measure the length and width of the quilt top.

2. Cut and piece together fabric to make the following: two yellow strips that measure 1½" by the length of the quilt top; two teal strips that measure 2½" by the length of the quilt top; and two multicolored strips that measure 4½" x the length of the quilt top.

3. Stitch one yellow, one teal and one multicolored strip together lengthwise, in that order, as shown. Repeat for the second set of strips. Press the seams to the outside.

4. Stitch one of the strip sets made in Step 3 to each side of the quilt top; place the yellow strip to the inside as shown in the Delightful Patches Bed Quilt Layout Diagram. Press the seams to the outside.

5. Cut and piece together fabric to make the following: two yellow strips that measure 1½" by the width of the quilt top, two teal strips that measure 2½" by the width of the quilt top; and two multicolored strips that measure 4½" by the width of the quilt top.

6. Stitch one yellow, one teal and one multicolored strip together lengthwise, in that order, as shown. Repeat for the second set of strips. Press the seams to the outside.

7. Stitch one lime green 7½" cornerstone square to each end of each strip set. Press the seams toward the middle.

8. Stitch one strip set to the top of the quilt top and another to the bottom of the quilt top; place the yellow strip to the inside as shown in the Layout Diagram. Press the seams to the outside.

FINISH

1. Layer the quilt top, batting and backing.

2. Quilt the piece as desired.

3. Bind the quilt with a narrow pink binding. See Chapter 1 for detailed instructions.

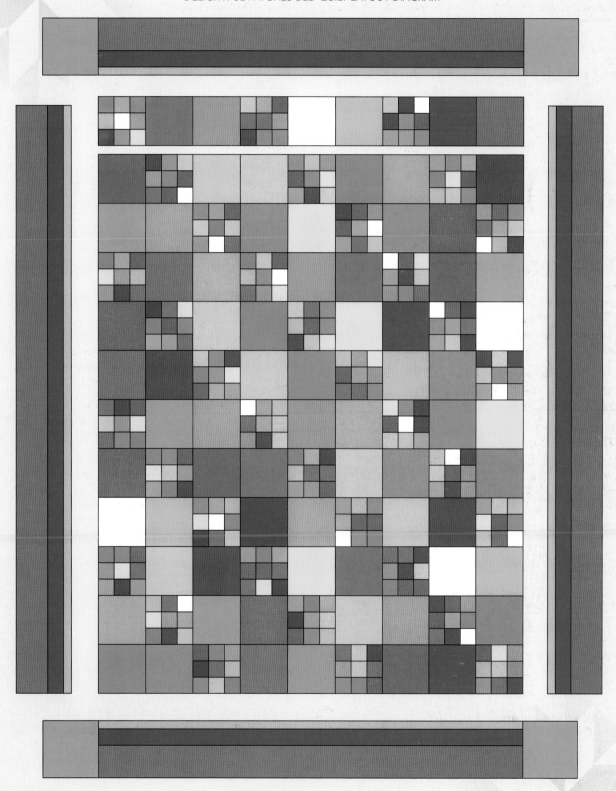

Handy-Dandy Wall Hanging

Every child needs a special place to put his or her favorite "stuff." This project provides a great place to store books, toys and other precious treasures. **Finished size: 26" x 26". Finished block size: 10" x 10".**

MATERIALS NEEDED

4 bright pastel fat quarters in light blue, light green, yellow and pink

½ yd. bright print (border)

¼ yd. fusible web

40-weight embroidery thread in hot pink, lime green, blue, golden yellow and orange*

Scraps of bright-colored fabrics

½ yd. pink (binding)

½ yd. cotton batting (pockets)

1 yd. batting (wall hanging)

1 yd. print (backing)

Thread

General sewing tools and supplies

* SULKY 40-WEIGHT EMBROIDERY THREADS NO. 1109, NO. 1024, NO. 1078, NO. 1196 AND NO. 1510 WERE USED FOR THE PROJECT SHOWN.

FABRIC	CUT	TO YIELD	FOR
Each of the 4 fat quarters	2 squares, 10½" x 10½"	8 squares	Background and pockets
Bright print	2 strips, 2½" x 10½"	2 strips	Borders
	3 strips, 2½" x 22½"	3 strips	Borders
	2 strips, 2½" x 26½"	2 strips	Borders
Cotton batting	4 pieces, 5" x 10¼"	4 pieces	Pockets

STITCH AND APPLIQUÉ

Pocket Blocks

1. Fold one square, right sides out, in half over one piece of cotton batting. Repeat to cover all four pieces of cotton batting.

2. Using the Circles patterns in the back of the book, trace four large, four medium and four small circles on the wrong side of fusible web. See Chapter 1 for detailed instructions on fusible appliqué.

3. Iron the fusible web circles to the wrong side of the fabric scraps. Cut out each circle on the traced lines.

4. Randomly position one circle of each size on each pocket. Fuse the circles in place; follow the manufacturer's directions.

5. Use a contrasting thread to zigzag stitch around the edges of the appliquéd circles as shown. Stitch through all of the layers; the zigzag stitching is the quilting for the pocket.

6. Lay one pocket on the bottom half of one 10½" square. Baste in place. Repeat for the remaining pockets.

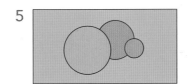

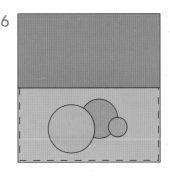

Borders

1. Stitch one 2½" x 10½" strip between two blocks as shown in the Handy-Dandy Wall Hanging Layout Diagram. Repeat. Press the seams toward the strips.

2. Stitch one 2½" x 22½" strip to the top of one two-pocket block set. Stitch one 2½" x 22½" strip to the bottom of the other two-pocket block set. Join the two pocket blocks together with one 2½" x 22½" strip as shown in the Layout Diagram. Press the seams toward the strips.

3. Stitch one 2½" x 26½" strip to each side of the four-pocket block; refer to the Layout Diagram. Press the seams toward the strips.

FINISH

1. Layer the quilt top, batting and backing.

2. Quilt the piece as desired.

3. Bind the quilt with a narrow pink binding. See Chapter 1 for detailed instructions.

4. Add a hanging sleeve to the quilt back, if desired.

HANDY-DANDY WALL HANGING LAYOUT DIAGRAM

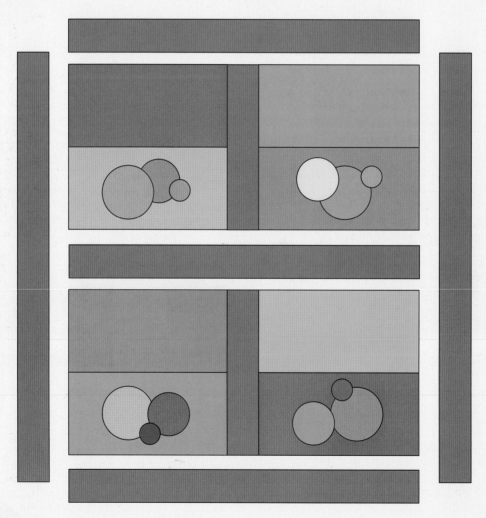

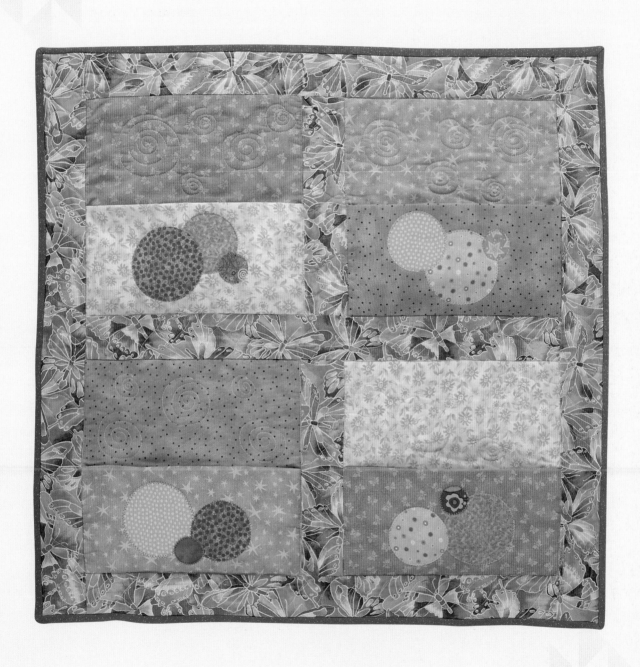

Fat Quarter Fun Pillowcases

You can whip up a pair of these pillowcases in a flash, each one only takes four fat quarters! They are so great for kids' gifts that I know all of my nieces and nephews will be getting them for Christmas. **Finished size: 20" x 30" which fits a standard-size pillowcase.**

MATERIALS NEEDED

(For one pillowcase)

4 fat quarters in various prints and colors (pillowcase)

1 yd. ribbon, ⅜" wide (trim)

General sewing tools and supplies

FABRIC	CUT	TO YIELD	FOR
All 3 fat quarters	Trim each fat quarter to 18" x 20"	3 rectangles	Pillowcase
1 of the 4 fat quarters	2 rectangles, 9" x 20"	2 rectangles	Pillowcase trim

STITCH

Pocket Blocks

1. Join together three fat quarters in a row, stitching the 20" sides together to create a rectangle that measures about 20" x 53". Press the seams open.

2. Fold the rectangle in half with right sides together so one and a half of the fat quarters are on each side of the fold as shown. Stitch the long edges together using a ¼" seam allowance.

3. Turn the piece right side out. Press.

4. Lay the two 9" x 20" pieces right sides together. Stitch along both 9" sides to form a tube.

5. Turn the tube right side out. Press.

6. Fold the pillowcase trim piece in half with right sides out so you still have a tube. Press.

7. Lay the pillowcase trim piece right sides together around the open end of the pillowcase, placing the folded edge of the trim back on the pillowcase body fabric. All three raw edges — two from the pillowcase trim and one from the pillowcase body — will meet. Stitch the raw edges together all the way around, ¼" from the edge. Avoid stitching the pillowcase shut.

8. Turn the trim piece right side out. Press the seam away from the pillowcase trim piece.

9. Lay a piece of ⅜" ribbon along the seam between the pillowcase and the trim. Fold the beginning and the ending of the ribbon under by ½". Zigzag stitch the ribbon in place.

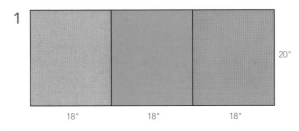

1 — 20" — 18" — 18" — 18"

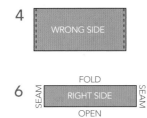

2 — WRONG SIDE — FOLD

4 — WRONG SIDE

6 — FOLD — RIGHT SIDE — SEAM — SEAM — OPEN

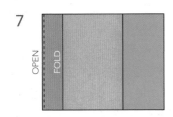

7 — OPEN — FOLD

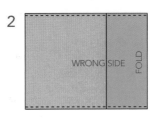

8

FAT QUARTER FUN PILLOWCASES
LAYOUT DIAGRAM

RIBBON

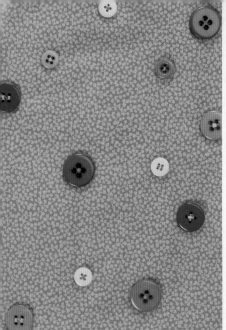

Jamming Pajama Tote

I know that I have a really hard time resisting a new purse, tote or bag. Regardless of your age, you never can have too many bags (or too much fabric, for that matter). This great little tote is perfect for your child to take her jammies to a sleepover. I hope that you have as much fun making it as I did. **Finished size: 13" x 14".**

MATERIALS NEEDED

4 fat quarters in pastel bright colors (handles, tote)

1 yd. rickrack trim

4 dozen bright buttons

Thread

General sewing tools and supplies

FABRIC	CUT		TO YIELD	FOR
Each fat quarter	1 strip, 2" x 20"		4 strips	Handles
	1 rectangle, 14½" x 16½"		4 rectangles	Tote

FAT QUARTER CUTTING DIAGRAM

STITCH

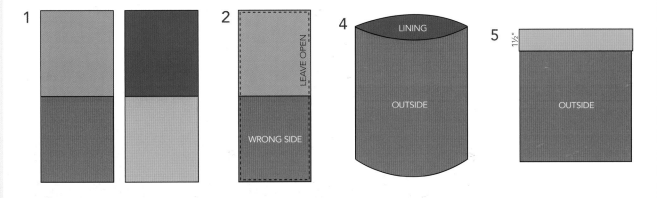

1. Sew two rectangles together, right sides together, along the 14½" side. Press the seams open. Repeat for the other two rectangles.

2. Lay the two sets of joined rectangles right sides together; line up the edges so they are even. Stitch all the way around, ¼" from the edge; leave an opening to turn the piece.

3. Turn the piece right side out. Slipstitch the opening closed.

4. Fold one half of the bag into the other; one half is the outside, and one half is the lining. Press around the opening at the top.

5. Fold the top edge down 1½" to form a cuff. Press the cuff in place.

6. Lay two 2" x 20" strips right sides together. Stitch both long edges; leave both short ends open to form a tube. Repeat for the second pair of 2" x 20" strips.

7. Turn each tube right side out. Press. Fold each tube's ends inside ¼". Topstitch each end closed.

8. Place a handle on the cuff, 3½" from each side of the tote. Line up each end of the handle with the edge of the cuff, and pin it in place. Repeat for the other handle on the other side of the bag. It doesn't matter which color is on which side.

6

7

8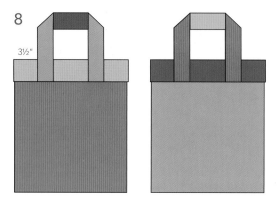

EMBELLISH

1. Lay a piece of rickrack trim on the middle of the cuff, all the way around the bag. Fold the beginning and end of the trim under ½". Stitch down the middle of the rickrack through all of the layers including the handles. Avoid sewing the tote shut.

2. Randomly sew buttons all over the sides of the tote.

1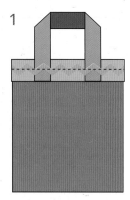

2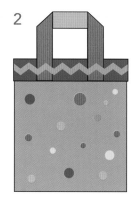

SEW A SENSATIONAL KITCHEN

SMALL FLOWER

TEAPOT

Patterns

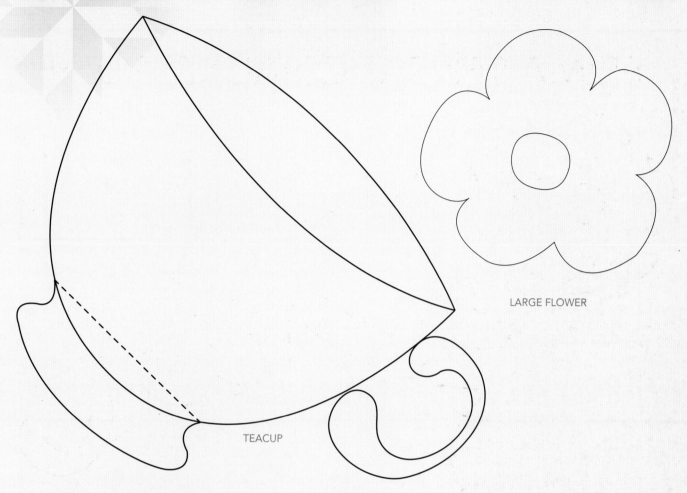

LARGE FLOWER

TEACUP

CREATE A COLORFUL KID'S ROOM

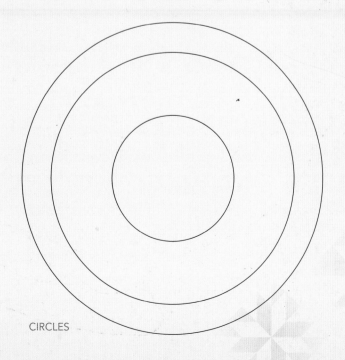

CIRCLES

Resources

Annie's Attic
1 Annie Lane
Big Sandy, TX 75755
Phone: (800) 582-6643
Web: www.anniesattic.com

Clotilde LLC
P.O. Box 7500
Big Sandy, TX 75755-7500
Phone: (800) 772-2891
Web: www.clotilde.com

Connecting Threads
P.O. Box 870760
Vancouver, WA 98687-7760
Phone: (800) 574-6454
Web: www.ConnectingThreads.com

Furniture & Appliancemart Superstore
Name-brand furniture, appliances, electronics and
bedding
3349 Church St.
Stevens Point, WI 54481
Phone: (715) 344-7700
Web: www.furnitureappliancemart.com

Herrschners Inc.
2800 Hoover Road
Stevens Point, WI 54492-0001
Phone: (800) 441-0838
Web: www.herrschners.com

Home Sew
P.O. Box 4099
Bethlehem, PA 18018-0099
Phone: (800) 344-4739
Web: www.homesew.com

KP Books
Publisher of this and other quality how-to books for
quilting, sewing and other crafts
700 E. State St.
Iola, WI 54990-0001
Phone: (888) 457-2873
Web: www.krause.com

Keepsake Quilting
Route 25
P.O. Box 1618
Center Harbor, NH 03226-1618
Phone: (800) 438-5464
Web: www.keepsakequilting.com

Nancy's Notions
333 Beichl Ave.
P.O. Box 683
Beaver Dam, WI 53916-0683
Phone: (800) 833-0690
Web: www.nancysnotions.com

Olfa-North America
Manufacturer of rotary cutters and mats
33 S. Sixth St.
Terre Haute, IN 47807
Phone: (800) 962-6532
Web: www.olfarotary.com

Penn's & Needles
124½ First St. W.
Mount Vernon, IA 52314
Phone: (319) 895-8063
Web: www.pennsandneedles.com

Prym-Dritz
Manufacturer of sewing, quilting and craft-related
notions, including Omnigrid rotary cutting equipment
P.O. Box 5028
Spartanburg, SC 29304
Web: www.prymdritz.com

Sulky of America, Inc.
Manufacturer of threads, stabilizers and spray
adhesives
Phone: (800) 874-4115 (to obtain a mail-order source)
Web: www.sulky.com

The Warm Company
Manufacturer of Warm & Natural batting, Steam-A-
Seam, Steam-A-Seam 2
954 East Union St.
Seattle, WA 98122
Phone: (800) 234-9276
Web: www.warmcompany.com

White Sewing Machines
Manufacturer of sewing machines, including Quilter's
Star model shown in book
31000 Viking Parkway
Westlake, OH 44145
Phone: (800) 331-3164
Web: www.whitesewing.com